Vegetarian

GENERAL EDITOR
CHUCK WILLIAMS

RECIPES
JOANNE WEIR

PHOTOGRAPHY
ALLAN ROSENBERG

TIME LIFE BOOKS

TIME-LIFE BOOKS
Time-Life Books is a division of Time Life Inc.
Time-Life is a trademark of Time Warner Inc. U.S.A.

A Note on Weights and Measures:
All recipes include customary U.S. and metric measurements. Metric conversions are based on a standard developed for these books and have been rounded off. Actual weights may vary.

Time-Life Custom Publishing
Vice President and Publisher: Terry Newell
Managing Editor: Donia Ann Steele
Director of New Product Development: Quentin McAndrew
Director of Sales: Neil Levin
Director of Financial Operations: J. Brian Birky

WILLIAMS-SONOMA
Founder/Vice-Chairman: Chuck Williams
Book Buyer: Victoria Kalish

WELDON OWEN INC.
President: John Owen
Publisher/Vice President: Wendely Harvey
Associate Publisher: Laurie Wertz
Managing Editor: Lisa Chaney Atwood
Consulting Editor: Norman Kolpas
Copy Editor: Sharon Silva
Design: John Bull, The Book Design Company
Production Director: Stephanie Sherman
Production Coordinator: Tarji Mickelson
Production Editor: Janique Gascoigne
Co-Editions Director: Derek Barton
Food Photographer: Allan Rosenberg
Additional Food Photography: Allen V. Lott
Primary Food Stylist: Heidi Gintner
Primary Prop Stylist: Sandra Griswold
Assistant Food Stylists: Nette Scott, Elizabeth C. Davis
Assistant Prop Stylist: Elizabeth C. Davis
Glossary Illustrations: Alice Harth

The Williams-Sonoma Kitchen Library
conceived and produced by Weldon Owen Inc.
814 Montgomery St., San Francisco, CA 94133

In collaboration with Williams-Sonoma
3250 Van Ness Ave., San Francisco, CA 94109

Printed in China

A Weldon Owen Production

Copyright © 1996 Weldon Owen Inc.
Reprinted 1996; 1996; 1996; 1997; 1997

Library of Congress
Cataloging-in-Publication Data:

Weir, Joanne.
　　Vegetarian / general editor, Chuck Williams ;
recipes, Joanne Weir; photography, Allan Rosenberg.
　　　p.　　cm. — (Williams-Sonoma kitchen library)
　　ISBN 0-7835-0311-3
　　1. Vegetarian　Cookery.　I. Williams, Chuck
II. Title.　III. Series.
TX837.W43　1996
641.5'636—dc20　　　　　　　95-32818
　　　　　　　　　　　　　　　　CIP

Contents

Soups & Salads 15

Main Courses 49

Side Dishes 93

INTRODUCTION

Just a few years ago, the word *vegetarian* conjured up exaggerated images of health fanatics living on spartan diets of nuts, grains and seeds.

But the world has changed. Today, menus found everywhere, from old-fashioned coffee shops to fashionable restaurants, proudly proclaim that vegetarian specialties are served—and even the most devoted meat eaters are likely to order them. Vegetarian dishes are featured in top food magazines and cookbooks, and home cooks don't hesitate to pair creative vegetable preparations with the best fresh produce their market has to offer.

Several factors explain these trends. Foremost, I think, is that people are more nutrition conscious in light of recent medical findings on the dangers of eating cholesterol-rich foods and the benefits of a high-fiber diet. Vegetables, grains and beans are all high in fiber and cholesterol free; and most grains and beans, when eaten together, provide complete dietary protein. At the same time, the widespread interest in quality cooking and dining has led to increased consumer demand for a first-rate selection of the finest and freshest vegetables—a demand now met by enterprising food stores and farmers' markets.

This book reflects these dramatic changes in the way we all eat. It begins with a comprehensive look at the basics of vegetarian cooking: kitchen equipment, step-by-step instructions for preparing a wide range of vegetables, and a selection of basic recipes for sauces, stocks and dressings. Following these fundamentals are 44 recipes, divided into sections on soups, salads, main dishes and side dishes. You can use this book to make up complete vegetarian menus, as well as to bring new variety to your nonvegetarian meals.

Seek out the best sources of vegetables in your area by asking friends or looking in the local newspaper's food section for information on farmers' markets. You'll be surprised at how wonderful your favorite vegetables will taste when they've been brought to you fresh from the harvest.

Chuck Williams

EQUIPMENT

A range of tools for chopping, slicing, shredding, cooking, puréeing and garnishing all kinds of vegetarian dishes

The array of kitchen equipment shown here reflects the delightful variety of vegetarian dishes. That variety stems both from the diversity to be found in the worlds of vegetables, grains and beans, and from the many methods by which all these ingredients can be cooked—simmering, sautéing, stewing, braising, baking and deep-frying.

1. Food Processor
For general chopping, slicing, shredding and puréeing of ingredients, particularly in large quantities.

2. Soufflé Dish
For baking and serving vegetable soufflés or puddings. Choose good-quality glazed porcelain, earthenware or ovenproof glass.

3. Baking Sheets
For roasting peppers, toasting nuts, and baking vegetable turnovers and pizzas.

4. Baking Pan
Square 9-inch (23-cm) metal pan used for all-purpose baking.

5. Tart Pan
Fluted 9-inch (23-cm) pan with removable bottom for easy shaping and unmolding of vegetable tarts.

6. Kitchen Towels
Good-quality cotton towels for general kitchen cleanup.

7. Measuring Cups and Spoons
Lip and handle on heavy-duty, heat-resistant glass measuring cups ensure easy pouring of liquid ingredients. Straight rims of calibrated metal spoons and cups in graduated sizes allow dry ingredients to be leveled for accuracy.

8. Mixing Bowls
Sturdy bowls in a range of sizes for mixing and serving. Can be made of earthenware, porcelain, glass or stainless steel.

9. Box Grater/Shredder
Sturdy stainless-steel tool for grating or shredding vegetables or cheeses by hand.

10. Biscuit Cutters
Sturdy, circular metal cutters in different sizes, for cutting out biscuit and turnover doughs and cooled-polenta rounds.

11. Ramekins
Individual ovenproof glass or ceramic dishes with ½-cup (4-fl oz/125-ml) capacity, for baking custards.

12. Baking Dishes
For baking or roasting vegetables, casseroles and pastas, and for providing a hot water bath in the oven for baked custards.

13. Metal Tongs
For handling deep-fried vegetarian specialties such as falafel,

and for quickly tossing spinach or other greens as they cook.

14. Deep-Fat Frying Thermometer
Suspended in a deep, heavy pot of hot oil, it accurately and quickly registers the temperature, allowing the cook to regulate heat levels for successful deep-frying.

15. Nutmeg Grater
Fine-rasped grater with a hinged flap that conceals a storage compartment for a whole nutmeg, allowing the spice to be freshly grated for each use.

16. Cheese Grater
Sturdy half-cylindrical model quickly grates hard cheeses such as Parmesan.

17. Slotted Spoon
For stirring sauces, casseroles and purées, and for removing and draining dumplings or vegetable pieces from the hot liquids or oil in which they have cooked.

18. Ricer
For puréeing some boiled or steamed vegetables, which are put in the basket of its lower half and forced through small holes when the hinged upper handle is closed. Choose a sturdy stainless-steel model. Particularly useful for potatoes, which become gummy if puréed in a food processor.

19. Mushroom Brush
Small brush with very soft bristles whisks away dirt from the surface of fresh mushrooms without blemishing them.

20. Vegetable Peeler
Double slotted blades thinly strip away vegetable peels.

21. Frying Pan
Choose good-quality, heavy aluminum, stainless steel, cast iron or enamel for rapid browning or frying of small quantities or pieces of vegetables. Sloped, shallow sides facilitate stirring or turning of vegetable pieces.

22. Blender
Variable-speed blender with heatproof glass bowl, for puréeing vegetable soups.

23. Electric Mixer
Heavy-duty, variable-speed countertop mixer with large mixing bowl and a variety of attachments.

24. Colander
For draining boiled or blanched vegetables and for draining off excess liquid from shredded and salted zucchini.

25. Assorted Kitchen Utensils
Crockery jar holds wooden spoons for general stirring, small wire whisk for mixing mayonnaise and other sauces, rubber spatula for folding beaten egg whites into soufflés, basting brush for brushing grilled vegetables with oil, and ladle for serving soups.

26. Saucepans
For boiling or braising vegetables, or for simmering sauces.

27. Hand-Held Electric Mixer
For beating egg whites when making savory soufflés.

28. Food Mill
Hand-turned crank forces boiled potatoes or other vegetables through one of two removable disks for coarser or finer purées; may be used to purée soups.

PREPARING FRESH VEGETABLES

Vegetables fall into so many categories—stalks and shoots, roots and tubers, leafy greens, mushrooms, vegetable-fruits such as tomatoes and eggplants—that numerous different preparation techniques naturally come into play. Some of the most common are demonstrated on the following pages. Please refer to the glossary on pages 104–107 for more information on vegetables.

REMOVING GRIT AND DIRT

Some vegetables, due to their growing conditions, hold significant amounts of grit and dirt, which must be carefully removed. Spinach, grown in sandy soil, or mushrooms, propagated in damp earth, call for special cleaning techniques.

Rinsing spinach leaves.
Fill a large bowl or sink with cold water and add the leaves—here, baby spinach. Slosh them around in the water to rinse thoroughly. Lift out the leaves and then discard the dirty water. Repeat the process until the water is perfectly clear when the leaves are removed.

Brushing fresh mushrooms.
Trim the mushroom stems, if necessary. Using a small, soft-bristled brush, such as the mushroom brush shown here, gently brush any dirt or grit from the surface of each mushroom. Do not rinse the mushrooms; contact with water can quickly turn them soggy.

HANDLING FRESH CHILI PEPPERS

The seeds and ribs of chili peppers are intensely hot, and many recipes call for their removal. After handling chilies, be sure to wash your hands well and take care not to touch your eyes or other sensitive areas.

Seeding chili peppers.
Wearing kitchen gloves to shield your hands from the volatile oils, use a small, sharp knife to halve each chili lengthwise. With your fingers or the knife, remove the stem. Using the knife tip, scrape out the seeds.

Couscous Salad with Cucumbers, Peppers and Red Onions

PEELING PEARL ONIONS

Part of the appeal of bite-sized pearl onions is that they can be cooked and eaten whole. A few simple steps must be performed when peeling the onions to ensure that they retain their shape during cooking.

1. Trimming the stem end.
Bring a saucepan three-fourths full of water to a boil. Meanwhile, use a small, sharp knife to trim off the root end of each pearl onion in a thin, even slice. Discard the root end.

2. Cutting a shallow X.
With the knife, cut a shallow X in the trimmed end of each pearl onion. This will help keep the layers from separating during cooking, so that the onion remains whole. Immerse the onions in the boiling water for about 2 minutes.

3. Slipping off the skin.
Drain the onions well. As soon as they are cool enough to handle, slip off the skin of each onion by gently squeezing the onion with your fingertips. Discard the skins and use the onions as directed in the recipe.

WORKING WITH CHEESE

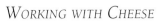

The way you prepare cheese for use in a recipe affects the end result. Shredded cheese melts evenly. Finely grated cheese blends in thoroughly. Cheese shavings make attractive garnishes.

Shredding semisoft to semi-hard cheeses.
Holding a large block of semi-soft to semihard cheese such as Monterey jack or Gouda, slide the cheese across the large holes of a cheese shredder or pass the cheese through the shredding attachment of a food processor.

Grating hard cheeses.
To grate a hard cheese such as Parmesan, draw it back and forth across the fine rasps of a hand-held grater, such as the half-cylindrical model shown here or the box model shown on page 6.

Shaving semihard cheeses.
To cut thin strips of a semi-hard cheese such as Gruyère, hold a block of the cheese in one hand and draw a vegetable peeler or cheese shaver—also known as a cheese plane—across the cheese.

The seeds and ribs of bell peppers (capsicums) are flavorless and indigestible and should be removed, as shown here, before the peppers are cut into quarters, strips or slices.

1. Halving the peppers.
Using a long, sharp knife, cut each bell pepper in half lengthwise through its stem end, exposing its inner cluster of seeds and its white ribs.

2. Removing the stems, seeds and ribs.
Using your fingers, pull out the stem section from each pepper half, along with the cluster of seeds attached to it. Remove any remaining seeds, along with any thin white membranes.

Roasted Pepper Salad with Garlic Bread

ROASTING & PEELING BELL PEPPERS

Roasting fresh bell peppers (capsicums) develops the sweet flavor and tender texture of their flesh, and also enables you to remove their skins easily.

1. Placing the peppers on a pan.
Preheat a broiler (griller). Cut the bell peppers lengthwise into halves and remove the stems, seeds and ribs as shown at left. Place the pepper halves on a broiler pan or baking sheet, cut sides down.

2. Roasting the peppers.
Broil the peppers until their skins blister and turn black. Remove the pan from the broiler (griller), drape the peppers loosely with aluminum foil, and let steam and cool for about 10 minutes.

3. Peeling the peppers.
When the peppers are cool enough to handle, uncover them and, using your fingertips or a small knife, peel off the blackened skins. Then tear or cut the peppers as directed in the recipe.

PEELING FRESH TOMATOES

Although tomatoes may simply be chopped or sliced before they are added to cooked vegetable dishes, often a recipe will call for peeling their shiny skins for a more refined end product. Brief contact with boiling water loosens the skins for easy peeling.

1. Scoring the skins.
Bring a saucepan three-fourths full of water to a boil. Meanwhile, use a small, sharp knife to cut out the core from the stem end of each tomato. Then cut a shallow X in the skin at the base of each tomato.

2. Loosening the skins.
Using a slotted spoon or wire skimmer, immerse the tomatoes in the boiling water for about 20 seconds. Then, using the spoon or skimmer, immediately submerge them in a bowl of cold water.

3. Peeling the tomatoes.
Starting at the X, peel the skin from each tomato, using your fingertips and, if necessary, the knife blade.

SEEDING TOMATOES

The watery seed sacs of a tomato contribute nothing to its flavor and can dilute the consistency of a dish in which they're included. An easy technique eliminates them.

1. Halving the tomatoes.
Use a sharp knife to cut out the stem end of each tomato. Cut each tomato in half crosswise, exposing its seed sacs.

2. Squeezing out seed sacs.
Grasp a tomato half in your cupped hand and hold it over a bowl or the sink. Squeeze gently to force out the seed sacs.

Vegetable Stock

A variety of vegetables can be used for making stock: leeks, carrots, celery, tomatoes, potatoes, mushrooms, green beans, squashes, fennel, broccoli, eggplant (aubergine), onions and greens such as spinach, Swiss chard and lettuce. Do not use cauliflower, Brussels sprouts, artichokes, beets or beet greens, as they are too strongly flavored.

10 cups (3 lb/1.5 kg) cut-up assorted fresh vegetables
   or vegetable trimmings (*see note*)
1 yellow onion, coarsely chopped
1 carrot, peeled and coarsely chopped
12 fresh parsley stems
pinch of fresh thyme leaves
1 bay leaf

*P*lace the assorted vegetables, onion and carrot in a stockpot. On the center of a small square of cheesecloth (muslin), place the parsley stems, thyme and bay leaf. Bring the corners together and tie securely with kitchen string to form a bundle. Add to the pot along with cold water to cover the vegetables by 3 inches (7.5 cm).

Bring to a boil over high heat, then immediately reduce the heat to low and simmer gently, uncovered, until the stock is aromatic and has a good flavor, 1–1½ hours. Add water as needed to maintain the original level.

Remove from the heat and pour the stock through a fine-mesh sieve into a clean container. Use immediately, or cover and refrigerate for up to 1 week or freeze for up to 2 months.

Makes 2–3 qt
(2–3 l)

Pesto

This smooth-textured pesto is made lighter by omitting the requisite pine nuts. If you wish to include them, add ¼ cup (1 oz/30 g) pine nuts to the blender or food processor with the basil.

1½ cups (1½ oz/45 g) lightly packed fresh basil leaves,
   carefully washed and well dried
¼ cup (¼ oz/7 g) fresh parsley leaves, carefully washed
   and well dried
4 cloves garlic, minced
½ cup (4 fl oz/125 ml) extra-virgin olive oil
1¼ cups (5 oz/155 g) freshly grated Parmesan cheese
salt and freshly ground pepper

*I*n a blender or a food processor fitted with the metal blade, combine the basil, parsley, garlic, olive oil and about half of the Parmesan cheese. Process for 1 minute, stopping and scraping down the sides of the container as needed, and continuing to process until smooth.

Add the remaining cheese and pulse a few times to combine. Season to taste with salt and pepper.

Makes about 1¼ cups (10 fl oz/310 ml)

Basil-Mint Pesto: Add 1 cup (1 oz/30 g) firmly packed, carefully washed and well-dried mint leaves with the basil and parsley.

Mayonnaise

When making mayonnaise, be sure that all ingredients are at room temperature, and do not add the oil too quickly or the mayonnaise will separate. Mayonnaise can also be made in a blender or a food processor fitted with the metal blade in basically the same way, adding the oil drop by drop with the motor running.

1 egg yolk
1 teaspoon Dijon-style mustard
⅓ cup (3 fl oz/80 ml) olive oil
⅓ cup (3 fl oz/80 ml) safflower oil or peanut oil
salt and freshly ground pepper
juice of ½ lemon

*I*n a bowl, whisk together the yolk, mustard and about 1 tablespoon of the olive oil until an emulsion forms. Combine the remaining olive oil and the safflower or peanut oil in a cup with a spout. Drop by drop, begin adding the oil mixture to the emulsion while whisking constantly. Continue to add the oil in this manner, whisking constantly and increasing the flow to a thin, steady stream as it is incorporated, until the mixture has the consistency of mayonnaise.

Season to taste with salt and pepper and the lemon juice.

Makes about 1 cup (8 fl oz/250 ml)

Garlic Mayonnaise: Add 3 cloves garlic, minced, to the finished mayonnaise and stir until well mixed.

Balsamic and Red Wine Vinegar Dressing

This versatile dressing is delicious with any salad of mixed greens, beans or legumes. To vary the flavor, use all red wine vinegar or all balsamic vinegar, as you wish. Then taste and adjust with more oil or vinegar, if needed. Be sure to whisk the dressing well just before using.

5 tablespoons (3 fl oz/80 ml) extra-virgin olive oil
1 tablespoon red wine vinegar
1 tablespoon balsamic vinegar
salt and freshly ground pepper

*I*n a small bowl, whisk together the olive oil, red wine vinegar and balsamic vinegar. Season to taste with salt and pepper.

Makes about ½ cup (4 fl oz/125 ml)

Butternut Squash–Carrot Soup

2 tablespoons olive oil

1 large yellow onion, chopped

1 butternut (pumpkin) squash, about
   1¼ lb (625 g), peeled, halved, seeded
   and coarsely chopped

3 large carrots, peeled and coarsely
   chopped

½ teaspoon sugar

1 teaspoon paprika

1¼ teaspoons ground cumin

¾ teaspoon ground turmeric

¾ teaspoon ground coriander

6 cups (48 fl oz/1.5 l) vegetable stock
   (*recipe on page 12*) or water

salt and freshly ground pepper

1 teaspoon water

½ cup (4 fl oz/125 ml) plain yogurt

⅓ cup (½ oz/15 g) chopped fresh
   cilantro (fresh coriander), including
   stems

1 tablespoon fresh lime juice

This exotic soup bursts with complex sweet and hot flavors. To make the soup fat-free, you can "sweat" the onions rather than sauté them. To do so, substitute ½ cup (4 fl oz/125 ml) water for the olive oil, cover the pan and cook the onions until soft, about 15 minutes. Then proceed with the recipe as directed. If you like, garnish each serving with a few paper-thin lime slices and whole cilantro leaves in place of the yogurt.

🌿

In a 4-qt (4-l) soup pot over medium-low heat, warm the olive oil. Add the onion and sauté, stirring occasionally, until soft, about 10 minutes. Add the squash, carrots and sugar and sauté, stirring, for 10 minutes. Add the paprika, cumin, turmeric and coriander and continue to sauté, stirring occasionally, for 10 minutes longer. Add the stock or water and bring to a boil over high heat. Reduce the heat to low and simmer, uncovered, until the squash and carrots are soft, 30–40 minutes. Remove from the heat and let cool slightly.

Working with 2 cups (16 fl oz/500 ml) of soup at a time, place in a blender and purée on high speed until very smooth and light, about 3 minutes. As each batch is puréed, transfer it to a large saucepan. If the soup is too thick, thin with a little water until it is the consistency of heavy (double) cream.

Place the soup over medium-high heat and warm to serving temperature. Season to taste with salt and pepper. Meanwhile, in a small bowl, whisk the water into the yogurt until smooth. Season to taste with salt and pepper.

To serve, stir the cilantro and lime juice into the soup, mixing well. Ladle the soup into warmed bowls and drizzle with the yogurt. Serve at once.

Serves 6

Warm Spinach Salad with Artichokes and Gruyère

2 lemons
12 small artichokes
6 fresh thyme sprigs
6 fresh parsley sprigs
2 bay leaves
10 cloves garlic
½ cup (4 fl oz/125 ml) olive oil
salt and freshly ground pepper
¾ lb (375 g) baby spinach leaves,
 carefully washed and well dried
balsamic and red wine vinegar dressing
 (recipe on page 13)
3 hard-cooked eggs, peeled and
 coarsely chopped
1 piece Gruyère cheese, 2 oz (60 g),
 shaved into paper-thin strips with
 a vegetable peeler or cheese shaver

*If pressed for time, skip the artichoke preparation below and use
1 can (12 oz/375 g) artichoke hearts in brine, drained and quartered.*

Using a vegetable peeler, remove the lemon zest from both lemons and place in a saucepan. Cut the lemons into halves and squeeze the juice into the same pan.

Working with 1 artichoke at a time, pull off the tough outer leaves until you reach the pale green leaves at the center. Cut off the top one-third of the artichoke and trim the stem even with the base. Add the artichoke to the saucepan. Toss gently to coat with the juice. Repeat with the remaining artichokes.

Add the thyme and parsley sprigs, bay leaves, garlic, olive oil and salt and pepper to taste. Add water just to cover the artichokes. Place a round piece of parchment paper the diameter of the pan directly on top of the artichokes to prevent them from browning. Bring the water to a boil over high heat. Reduce the heat to medium-low and simmer the artichokes until they just begin to soften, about 5 minutes. Turn off the heat and let cool.

Meanwhile, place the spinach in a large bowl.

When the artichokes have cooled, drain and cut them lengthwise into quarters. In a frying pan over medium heat, combine the artichokes and dressing and heat, stirring occasionally, until the artichokes are warm, about 2 minutes. Remove from the heat and season to taste with salt and pepper.

Add the artichokes and dressing to the spinach and toss to mix. Immediately transfer to a large serving bowl or individual plates. Garnish with the chopped egg and Gruyère. Serve at once.

Serves 6

Spring Vegetable Soup with Basil-Mint Pesto

½ cup (3½ oz/105 g) dried small white (navy) beans

2 tablespoons extra-virgin olive oil

1 yellow onion, chopped

2 carrots, peeled and cut into ½-inch (12-mm) dice

2 celery stalks, cut into ½-inch (12-mm) dice

2 cups (12 oz/375 g) peeled, seeded and chopped plum (Roma) tomatoes (fresh or canned)

1 tablespoon tomato paste

8 cups (64 fl oz/2 l) vegetable stock (*recipe on page 12*) or water

½ lb (250 g) green beans, trimmed and cut into 1-inch (2.5-cm) lengths

¼ lb (125 g) dried penne pasta or small elbow macaroni

1 bunch Swiss chard, carefully washed, leaves and stems cut into 1-inch (2.5-cm) pieces

salt and freshly ground pepper

basil-mint pesto (*recipe on page 12*)

Pesto brings out the fresh character of this soup. You can top each bowl with a spoonful of pesto before serving as directed, or pass it in a small bowl at the table for guests to help themselves.

❧

Pick over the white beans and discard any misshapen beans or stones. Rinse the beans and drain. Place in a bowl, add plenty of water to cover and let soak for 3 hours.

Drain the beans and place them in a saucepan with water to cover by 2 inches (5 cm). Bring to a boil over high heat. Reduce the heat to medium-low and simmer, uncovered, until almost tender, 30–40 minutes. Drain and set aside.

In a 4-qt (4-l) soup pot over medium-low heat, warm the olive oil. Add the onion, carrots and celery and sauté, stirring, until the vegetables are soft, about 25 minutes. Add the tomatoes, tomato paste, stock or water and reserved white beans and simmer, uncovered, for 25 minutes.

Add the green beans and pasta, cover and simmer until the pasta is tender, about 15 minutes. Add the Swiss chard and simmer until it wilts, about 5 minutes. Season to taste with salt and pepper.

Ladle the soup into warmed bowls and place a large spoonful of pesto on top of each serving. Serve at once.

Serves 6

Grilled Vegetable Salad

3 slender (Asian) eggplants (aubergines)
6 small tomatoes
1 large red bell pepper (capsicum)
1 large green bell pepper (capsicum)
2 small yellow onions
salt and freshly ground pepper
3 tablespoons extra-virgin olive oil
3 tablespoons chopped fresh parsley
2 cloves garlic, minced
12 Kalamata or Niçoise olives, well
   drained

This dish is best when made in the late summer or early fall at the peak of the vegetable harvest. When no charcoal grill is available, char the vegetables under a broiler (griller) or directly over the flame of the burners on a gas stove. Garnish with a few slices of toasted bread, rubbed with garlic and brushed with fruity olive oil, if you like.

Prepare a fire in a charcoal grill. Preheat an oven to 350°F (180°C).

When the fire is very hot, place the eggplants, tomatoes, bell peppers and onions on the grill rack and grill, turning occasionally, until they are blackened on all sides, about 10 minutes.

Transfer the vegetables to a baking sheet and place in the oven. Bake until soft; the eggplants, tomatoes and bell peppers will be ready in about 20 minutes and the onions will take about 1 hour. When the vegetables are done, place them in a plastic or paper bag, close tightly and let stand until cool enough to handle.

Remove the vegetables from the bag. Stem, seed, derib and peel the bell peppers, then slice into long, narrow strips. Trim off the stem from each eggplant and peel off the skin; tear the flesh into long, thin strips. Peel and thinly slice the onions. Slip the skins off the tomatoes and cut the tomatoes lengthwise into quarters.

Place the vegetables on a serving dish, arranging them in alternating stripes of color. Season to taste with salt and pepper. Drizzle with the olive oil. In a small bowl, stir together the parsley and garlic and then sprinkle the mixture over the vegetables. Garnish with the olives and serve.

Serves 6

Corn, Bell Pepper and Potato Chowder

2 tablespoons unsalted butter

2 yellow onions, coarsely chopped

1 small carrot, peeled and coarsely chopped

2 yellow bell peppers (capsicums), seeded, deribbed and coarsely chopped

¼ teaspoon fresh thyme leaves

6 cups (48 fl oz/1.5 l) vegetable stock (*recipe on page 12*) or water

kernels from 6 ears of corn or 4–5 cups (about 1½ lb/750 g) frozen corn kernels

½ lb (250 g) russet potatoes, peeled and cut into ½-inch (12-mm) dice

1 cup (8 fl oz/250 ml) milk

salt and freshly ground pepper

2 tablespoons finely chopped fresh chives or green (spring) onions

If you would like a heartier soup, add 3 more small bell peppers, either all of the same color or 1 red, 1 green and 1 yellow. Cut all the peppers into halves and remove the seeds and ribs, then cut into ½-inch (12-mm) squares and sauté in 1 tablespoon olive oil until soft. Add the sautéed peppers to the puréed soup along with the corn and potatoes.

❧

*I*n a 4-qt (4-l) soup pot over medium-low heat, melt the butter. Add the yellow onions, carrot, bell peppers and thyme and sauté, stirring occasionally, until the vegetables are soft, about 15 minutes.

Add the stock or water and half of the corn and bring to a boil over medium-high heat. Reduce the heat to low and simmer, uncovered, until the vegetables are very soft, about 20 minutes. Remove from the heat and let cool slightly. Working with 2 cups (16 fl oz/500 ml) of soup at a time, place in a blender and purée on high speed until very smooth and light, about 3 minutes. As each batch is puréed, transfer it to a large saucepan.

Place the soup over medium heat and bring to a simmer. Add the potatoes and the remaining corn and simmer, uncovered, until the potatoes are soft when pierced with a fork, about 15 minutes. Pour in the milk, stir well and return to a simmer. Season to taste with salt and pepper.

Ladle into warmed bowls and garnish with the chives or green onions. Serve immediately.

Serves 6

Warm Red Cabbage, Red Onion and Apple Slaw

½ head red cabbage

5 tablespoons (3 fl oz/80 ml) extra-virgin olive oil

1 large red (Spanish) onion, cut into 8 wedges

2 tart green apples, such as pippin or Granny Smith, each cut into 8 wedges and cored

1 teaspoon caraway seeds

3 tablespoons balsamic vinegar

salt and freshly ground pepper

To dress up this simple slaw, top it with crumbled fresh goat cheese or blue or feta cheese. A few sprigs of flat-leaf (Italian) parsley make an attractive contrasting garnish.

Cut away the core from the cabbage half. Cut the cabbage into ½-by-2-inch (12-mm-by-5-cm) pieces. Set aside.

In a large frying pan over medium heat, warm the olive oil. Add the onion and sauté, stirring occasionally, until hot, about 2 minutes. Add the cabbage, apples, caraway seeds and vinegar and stir well. Continue to cook uncovered, stirring occasionally, until the cabbage softens, about 4 minutes. Season to taste with salt and pepper.

Transfer to a warmed platter and serve immediately.

Serves 6

Chilled Curried Potato-Leek Soup

2 tablespoons unsalted butter

2 yellow onions, chopped

3 leeks, white part and 1 inch (2.5 cm) of the green, halved lengthwise, carefully washed and sliced crosswise

1 clove garlic, minced

1 tablespoon curry powder

3 cups (24 fl oz/750 ml) vegetable stock (*recipe on page 12*) or water

4 red potatoes, about 1 lb (500 g) total weight, peeled and thinly sliced

1 teaspoon salt, plus salt to taste

3 cups (24 fl oz/750 ml) milk, or as needed

freshly ground pepper

2 tablespoons finely chopped fresh chives

Creamy puréed potatoes give this light summer soup extra body. Herbed croutons can be used as a garnish in addition to the chives.

In a 4-qt (4-l) soup pot over medium-low heat, melt the butter. Add the onions and leeks and sauté, stirring, until the vegetables begin to soften, about 5 minutes. Add the garlic and curry powder and sauté, stirring occasionally, until the onions and leeks are soft, about 10 minutes. Add the vegetable stock or water, potatoes and the 1 teaspoon salt. Cover and cook until the potatoes are soft when pierced with a fork, about 20 minutes.

Pour in the 3 cups (24 fl oz/750 ml) milk and stir to mix well. Working with 2 cups (16 fl oz/500 ml) of soup at a time, place in a blender and purée on high speed until very smooth and light, about 3 minutes. As each batch is puréed, transfer it to a large bowl. If the soup is too thick, add more milk and stir until the soup is the consistency of heavy (double) cream. Cover and chill for 2 hours.

Season to taste with salt and pepper. Ladle into chilled bowls and garnish with the chives. Serve immediately.

Serves 6

Couscous Salad with Cucumber, Peppers and Tomatoes

1 cup (8 fl oz/250 ml) water
1 cup (6 oz/185 g) couscous
½ teaspoon salt, plus salt to taste
2 green bell peppers (capsicums)
½ lb (250 g) cherry tomatoes, halved
1 cucumber, peeled, halved lengthwise, seeded and cut into ½-inch (12-mm) dice
1 small fresh red or green jalapeño or serrano chili pepper, seeded and minced
⅓ cup (½ oz/15 g) chopped fresh cilantro (fresh coriander)
6 tablespoons (3 fl oz/90 ml) extra-virgin olive oil
5 tablespoons (2½ fl oz/80 ml) fresh lemon juice
1½ teaspoons ground cumin
½ teaspoon paprika
3 cloves garlic, minced
freshly ground pepper

This zesty salad is a delicious light meal on its own, but it can also be tucked into a halved pita bread with shredded lettuce or sliced avocado to serve as a sandwich. It can be made up to 2 hours in advance; cover and refrigerate until you are ready to serve.

Preheat a broiler (griller).

In a saucepan, bring the water to a boil. Remove from the heat and add the couscous and the ½ teaspoon salt. Stir well, cover and let stand for 10 minutes. Uncover and transfer the couscous to a large, shallow baking dish, fluffing with a fork and spreading it evenly. Let cool completely.

Cut the bell peppers in half lengthwise and remove the stems, seeds and ribs. Place cut sides down on a baking sheet. Broil (grill) until the skins blacken and blister (see page 10). Remove the baking sheet from the broiler, drape the peppers loosely with aluminum foil and let cool for 10 minutes. Using your fingers or a small knife, remove the pepper skins. Cut the peppers into ½-inch (12-mm) squares.

Transfer the couscous to a large bowl. Scatter the bell peppers, tomatoes, cucumber, chili pepper and cilantro over the top.

In a small bowl, whisk together the olive oil, lemon juice, cumin, paprika and garlic. Season to taste with salt and pepper. Add to the couscous and toss together well. Before serving, taste and adjust the seasoning, if necessary.

Serves 6

Salad of Warm Roasted Beets, Green Beans and Olives

1½ lb (750 g) beets (8–10 beets),
   unpeeled and well scrubbed
1 tablespoon extra-virgin olive oil
¼ cup (2 fl oz/60 ml) water
salt
½ lb (250 g) green beans
1 cup (8 fl oz/250 ml) mayonnaise
   (recipe on page 13)
2 cloves garlic, minced
2 tablespoons warm water
¼ red (Spanish) onion, thinly sliced
½ cup (2½ oz/75 g) well-drained
   Kalamata or Niçoise olives
freshly ground pepper
lemon wedges

Tiny roasted potatoes make a great addition to this salad. To roast the potatoes, follow the procedure for the beets, but omit the water from the baking pan. Whole fresh basil leaves or thyme sprigs make a nice garnish.

Preheat an oven to 350°F (180°C).

Place the beets in a 9-by-13-inch (23-by-33-cm) baking dish. Drizzle evenly with the olive oil and the water. Cover with aluminum foil and bake until the beets can be easily pierced with a skewer, 1–1¼ hours.

About 15 minutes before the beets are done, fill a large saucepan three-fourths full with water, salt it lightly, and bring to a boil over high heat. Add the beans and cook until tender when pierced with the tip of a knife, 10–12 minutes. Drain immediately and keep warm.

In a small bowl, whisk together the mayonnaise, garlic and warm water to form a barely fluid sauce. Set aside.

When the beets are cooked, remove from the oven, remove the foil and let the beets stand just until cool enough to handle. Then peel the beets and cut into slices ¼ inch (6 mm) thick.

To serve, place the warm beets on a large platter. Top with the warm green beans. Scatter the onion and olives on top and season to taste with salt and pepper. Drizzle the vegetables with the mayonnaise sauce and garnish with the lemon wedges. Serve at once.

Serves 6

Greens and Farfalle Soup

2 tablespoons extra-virgin olive oil

3 cloves garlic, finely chopped

small pinch of red pepper flakes

8 cups (64 fl oz/2 l) vegetable stock
(recipe on page 12)

¼ lb (125 g) dried farfalle pasta

¼ lb (125 g) escarole, carefully washed
and cut into 1-inch (2.5-cm) pieces

¼ lb (125 g) Swiss chard, stemmed,
carefully washed and cut into 1-inch
(2.5-cm) pieces

2 teaspoons fresh lemon juice

salt and freshly ground pepper

¾ cup (3 oz/90 g) freshly grated
Parmesan cheese

Small elbow macaroni, penne, orzo or fusilli can replace the farfalle in this hearty soup. And, if you like, you can also substitute greens such as spinach, turnip greens, beet greens or kale for the escarole and Swiss chard.

❧

In a 4-qt (4-l) soup pot over medium-low heat, warm the olive oil. Add the garlic and red pepper flakes and cook, stirring constantly, until the garlic is soft but not golden, about 2 minutes. Add the stock and bring to a boil over high heat. Add the pasta, reduce the heat to medium and simmer, uncovered, until the pasta is cooked, 12–15 minutes.

Add the escarole and Swiss chard, stir well and continue to simmer just until the greens wilt but are still bright green, about 3 minutes. Remove from the heat and add the lemon juice and season to taste with salt and pepper.

Ladle into warmed bowls and serve immediately. Pass the Parmesan cheese at the table.

Serves 6

Tabbouleh

1 cup (6 oz/185 g) medium-fine bulgur

⅔ cup (5 fl oz/160 ml) extra-virgin olive oil

1 cup (8 fl oz/250 ml) fresh lemon juice, plus lemon juice to taste

5 cloves garlic, minced

1 teaspoon salt, plus salt to taste

6 green (spring) onions, including tender green tops, cut into slices ¼ inch (6 mm) thick

2 large bunches fresh parsley, stemmed and chopped

⅓ cup (½ oz/15 g) chopped fresh mint

5 large tomatoes, cut into ¼-inch (6-mm) dice

2 cucumbers, peeled, halved lengthwise, seeded and cut into ¼-inch (6-mm) dice

freshly ground pepper

pita breads, warmed, or romaine (cos) lettuce leaves

For a light, healthful lunch, serve this popular Middle Eastern salad alongside a bowl of spring vegetable soup with basil-mint pesto (recipe on page 19) or butternut squash–carrot soup (page 15) and wedges of pita bread.

❧

Place the bulgur in the bottom of a large salad bowl. In a small bowl, whisk together the olive oil, the 1 cup (8 fl oz/ 250 ml) lemon juice, garlic and the 1 teaspoon salt. Pour over the bulgur and toss well. Layer on top of the bulgur, in the following order, the green onions, parsley, mint, tomatoes and cucumbers. Season the cucumbers well with salt and pepper and cover the bowl with plastic wrap. Refrigerate for at least 24 hours or for up to 48 hours.

Bring the salad to room temperature. Toss the ingredients together, then taste and adjust the seasoning with additional salt, pepper and lemon juice, if necessary. Serve with pita bread or romaine lettuce leaves to use for scooping up the salad.

Serves 6–8

Italian Bread Salad with Tomatoes and Basil

1 small loaf country-style bread, ½ lb (250 g), a few days old

1 cup (8 fl oz/250 ml) water

6 ripe tomatoes, seeded *(see page 11)* and cut into ½-inch (12-mm) dice

1 small red (Spanish) onion, thinly sliced

1 cucumber, peeled, halved lengthwise, seeded and cut into ½-inch (12-mm) dice

2 cloves garlic, minced

3 tablespoons well-drained capers

½ cup (½ oz/15 g) lightly packed fresh basil leaves, carefully washed and torn into pieces

1 cup (8 fl oz/250 ml) balsamic and red wine vinegar dressing *(recipe on page 13)*

salt and freshly ground pepper

In Italy, yesterday's stale bread is sometimes made into today's fresh and flavorful panzanella *salad. Make sure to use a good-quality country-style bread for this salad—the coarser the better. Loaves made with unbleached flour are ideal, although those that also include whole-wheat or rye flour may also be used.*

Cut the bread crosswise into slices 1 inch (2.5 cm) thick. Place in a large shallow container and pour the water evenly over the slices. Let stand for 1 minute. Carefully squeeze the bread between your hands until dry. Tear the bread into rough 1-inch (2.5-cm) pieces and spread out on paper towels to absorb any excess moisture for 10 minutes.

In a bowl, combine the tomatoes, onion, cucumber, garlic, capers, basil and bread. Toss together to mix well. Add the dressing and toss again until evenly distributed. Cover and let rest in the refrigerator for 1 hour.

Season to taste with salt and pepper. Transfer to a platter or individual plates and serve.

Serves 6

Lentil Salad with Red Pepper, Mint and Feta

1 cup (7 oz/220 g) dried lentils

5 tablespoons (3 fl oz/80 ml) extra-
virgin olive oil

5 tablespoons (3 fl oz/80 ml) red wine
vinegar, plus vinegar to taste

2 cloves garlic, minced

½ teaspoon ground cumin

salt and freshly ground pepper

1 small red (Spanish) onion, diced

1 red bell pepper (capsicum), seeded,
deribbed and finely diced

¼ cup (¼ oz/7 g) chopped fresh mint,
plus mint sprigs for garnish

6 oz (185 g) feta cheese, crumbled

Lentils, like most beans, are a terrific source of protein. Look for green lentils in well-stocked food stores or replace them with your favorite dried beans; soak and cook the dried beans first, then add them warm to the oil and vinegar mixture. You might try small white (navy), pinto or black beans, or chick-peas (garbanzo beans). Fresh goat cheese can be substituted for the feta. Kalamata olives make a tasty, attractive garnish.

❧

Pick over the lentils and discard any misshapen lentils and stones. Rinse the lentils and drain, then transfer to a sauce-pan and add water to cover by 2 inches (5 cm). Bring to a boil over high heat. Reduce the heat to medium-low and simmer, uncovered, until the lentils are tender, 15–20 minutes. Remove from the heat, drain immediately and place in a bowl.

In a small bowl, whisk together the olive oil, the 5 table-spoons (3 fl oz/80 ml) vinegar, garlic, cumin and salt and pepper to taste. Add to the warm lentils and toss together to coat evenly. Add the onion and bell pepper and toss gently. Let stand for 20 minutes at room temperature.

Season to taste with more salt, pepper and vinegar, if necessary. Add the mint and toss to mix well. Transfer the salad to a platter or individual plates. Sprinkle with the feta, garnish with mint sprigs and serve.

Serves 6

Cauliflower and Cheddar Cheese Soup

2 small heads cauliflower, 2½ lb
   (1.25 kg) total weight
salt
2 tablespoons unsalted butter
1 large yellow onion, chopped
1 clove garlic, minced
4 cups (32 fl oz/1 l) vegetable stock
   (*recipe on page 12*) or water
1 teaspoon dry mustard
pinch of freshly grated nutmeg
1½ cups (12 fl oz/375 ml) milk
2 cups (8 oz/250 g) coarsely shredded
   sharp white Cheddar cheese
freshly ground pepper
2 tablespoons sliced green (spring)
   onions

This soup is also delicious made with fresh corn kernels, broccoli, butternut (pumpkin) squash, acorn squash or pumpkin in place of the cauliflower and garnished with Gruyère instead of Cheddar.

❧

*T*rim the cauliflowers. Cut 1 of the cauliflower heads into ½-inch (12-mm) florets. Fill a saucepan three-fourths full with water, salt it lightly and bring to a boil over high heat. Add the florets, reduce the heat to medium-low and simmer until tender when pierced with a fork, 10–12 minutes. Drain well; set aside. Cut the remaining cauliflower head into 2-inch (5-cm) pieces; set aside.

In a 4-qt (4-l) soup pot over medium-low heat, melt the butter. Add the onion and sauté, stirring, until soft, about 10 minutes. Add the garlic and sauté, stirring, for 2 minutes longer.

Add the stock or water, reserved raw cauliflower pieces, dry mustard and nutmeg and bring to a boil over high heat. Reduce the heat to low and simmer, uncovered, until the cauliflower is soft, about 30 minutes. Remove from the heat and cool slightly.

Working with 2 cups (16 fl oz/500 ml) of soup at a time, place in a blender and blend at high speed until very smooth and light, about 3 minutes. As each batch is puréed, transfer it to a clean, large saucepan. Place the soup over medium-low heat, pour in the milk and stir well. Bring the soup to a simmer and add the reserved cooked florets and 1½ cups (6 oz/185 g) of the cheese. Stir well until the cheese melts and the soup is hot, about 5 minutes. Season to taste with salt and pepper.

Ladle the soup into warmed bowls. Sprinkle evenly with the remaining ½ cup (2 oz/65 g) cheese and the green onions. Serve immediately.

Serves 6

Baked Goat Cheese with Salad Greens

3 small rounds fresh goat cheese, each
  about ¼ lb (125 g), 2½ inches (6 cm)
  in diameter and 1 inch (2.5 cm) thick
2 tablespoons extra-virgin olive oil
balsamic and red wine vinegar dressing
  (recipe on page 13)
1 clove garlic, minced
salt and freshly ground pepper
1½ cups (6 oz/185 g) fine dried bread
  crumbs
4 large handfuls mesclun or mixed salad
  greens (see note), torn into large bite-
  sized pieces, carefully washed and
  well dried

This salad is inspired by one served at the well-known Chez Panisse restaurant in Berkeley, California. Select a mixture of salad greens that include red leaf lettuce, radicchio, butter lettuce, mustard greens, frisée, mizuna, arugula (rocket) and/or oak leaf lettuce in any combination. If you like, garnish the salad with slices of different colored roasted bell peppers (capsicums), brine-cured black olives, or herbed and garlic-flavored croutons. Accompany with slices of good crusty bread.

❧

Preheat an oven to 400°F (200°C).

Cut each cheese round in half horizontally to make 6 rounds in all. Place on a plate and drizzle with the olive oil, turning once to lightly coat both sides. Set aside.

In a small bowl, whisk together the dressing, garlic and salt and pepper to taste. Set aside.

Spread the bread crumbs on a plate. Coat the rounds of goat cheese on both sides with the crumbs and then place well spaced on a baking sheet. Bake until the cheese rounds are slightly bubbling around the edges, 4–6 minutes.

Place the greens in a bowl and drizzle with the dressing. Toss well and divide the greens evenly among 6 salad plates. Place a hot cheese round in the center of each mound of greens. Serve immediately.

Serves 6

Roasted Pepper Salad with Garlic Bread

4 large red bell peppers (capsicums)
4 large yellow bell peppers (capsicums)
¼ cup (2 fl oz/60 ml) balsamic and
   red wine vinegar dressing (recipe on
   page 13)
salt and freshly ground pepper
½ cup (3 oz/90 g) caper berries
   (see note)
⅓ cup (2 oz/60 g) well-drained
   Kalamata or Niçoise olives
½ cup (½ oz/15 g) lightly packed basil
   leaves
6 slices country-style bread
2 cloves garlic

Caper berries are larger than regular capers—about the size of an olive or small cherry—and have long stems. Look for them in Italian delicatessens and specialty-food stores. Substitute ¼ cup (2 oz/60 g) regular capers, if unavailable.

❧

Preheat a broiler (griller). Cut the bell peppers in half lengthwise and remove the stems, seeds and ribs. Place cut sides down on a baking sheet. Broil (grill) until the skins blacken and blister (see page 10). Remove the baking sheet from the broiler, drape the peppers loosely with aluminum foil and let cool for 10 minutes. Using your fingers or a small knife, remove the pepper skins. Cut the peppers lengthwise into strips 1 inch (2.5 cm) wide and place in a bowl.

  Add the dressing and salt and pepper to taste and toss well. Arrange the peppers on a platter or individual plates and scatter the caper berries, olives and basil over the top.

  Toast the bread until lightly golden on both sides. Lightly rub the garlic cloves over one side of each bread slice.

  Tuck the garlic bread slices alongside the salad and serve.

Serves 6

Grilled Vegetable Skewers with Romesco Sauce

FOR THE SAUCE:

4 tablespoons (2 fl oz/60 ml) extra-
  virgin olive oil
2 slices coarse-textured white bread
¼ cup (1½ oz/45 g) blanched almonds
1 cup (6 oz/185 g) peeled, seeded and
  chopped tomatoes (fresh or canned)
1 clove garlic, minced
2 teaspoons sweet paprika
¼ teaspoon red pepper flakes
3 tablespoons red wine vinegar
salt and freshly ground pepper

6 slender (Asian) eggplants (aubergines),
  1 lb (500 g) total weight, cut crosswise
  into slices ¾ inch (2 cm) thick
24 fresh whole mushrooms, 1 lb (500 g)
  total weight, brushed clean
6 long, thin zucchini, 1¼ lb (625 g)
  total weight, cut crosswise into slices
  1 inch (2.5 cm) thick
12 cherry tomatoes
3 tablespoons olive oil for brushing
flat-leaf (Italian) parsley sprigs, optional

In Spain, the zesty almond-pepper sauce known as romesco is a classic accompaniment to grilled fish, although it is equally delicious spooned over vegetables. Romesco is also good served with crispy polenta triangles (recipe on page 53) in place of the saffron tomatoes.

To make the sauce, in a frying pan over medium heat, warm 2 tablespoons of the olive oil. Add the bread and fry, turning once or twice with tongs, until golden on both sides, about 2 minutes. Transfer the bread to a food processor fitted with the metal blade.

Add the almonds to the oil remaining in the frying pan and sauté, stirring, until golden, about 2 minutes. Transfer the almonds to the processor, along with the tomatoes, garlic, paprika and red pepper flakes. In a small cup, combine the red wine vinegar and the remaining 2 tablespoons olive oil. With the processor motor running, pour in the olive oil mixture in a slow, steady stream. Season to taste with salt and pepper. Pour the sauce into a serving bowl and let stand for 1 hour before serving.

Place 12 bamboo skewers in water to cover for 30 minutes. Prepare a fire in a charcoal grill.

Drain the skewers. Thread the eggplant slices, mushrooms, zucchini slices and tomatoes onto the skewers, alternating the vegetables and distributing them evenly among the skewers. Brush the vegetables with the olive oil.

When the fire is ready, place the skewers on the grill rack and grill, turning occasionally, until tender when pierced with a fork, 10–15 minutes.

Place 2 skewers on each serving plate and garnish with parsley sprigs, if desired. Pass the sauce at the table.

Serves 6

Mushroom Barley Stew with Biscuit Crust

FOR THE STEW:

¾ cup (5 oz/155 g) dried chick-peas
   (garbanzo beans)

2 tablespoons vegetable oil or olive oil

18 pearl onions, peeled (*see page 9*)

4 carrots, peeled and cut into 1½-inch
   (4-cm) lengths

2 celery stalks, cut into 1½-inch (4-cm)
   lengths

2 tablespoons all-purpose (plain) flour

6 cups (48 fl oz/1.5 l) vegetable stock
   (*recipe on page 12*)

1 teaspoon dried herbes de Provence

3 cloves garlic, minced

⅓ cup (2½ oz/75 g) pearl barley

¾ lb (375 g) red potatoes, quartered

1 cup (3 oz/90 g) sugar snap peas,
   trimmed

¾ lb (375 g) fresh white mushrooms,
   brushed clean and halved

salt and freshly ground pepper

FOR THE BISCUITS:

2½ cups (12½ oz/390 g) all-purpose
   (plain) flour, plus extra for dusting

1 teaspoon salt

1 tablespoon baking powder

½ cup (4 oz/125 g) unsalted butter,
   at room temperature, cut into
   tablespoon-sized pieces

1 cup (8 fl oz/250 ml) buttermilk,
   at room temperature

*T*o make the stew, pick over the chick-peas and discard any misshapen peas or stones. Rinse the chick-peas and drain. Place in a bowl, add plenty of water to cover and let soak for 3 hours.

Drain the chick-peas and place in a saucepan with water to cover by 2 inches (5 cm). Bring to a boil over high heat. Reduce the heat to medium-low and simmer, uncovered, until tender, 45–60 minutes. Drain and set aside.

In a soup pot over medium heat, warm the oil. Add the chick-peas, pearl onions, carrots and celery and stir briefly. Sift the flour over the vegetables. Cook, stirring, for 2 minutes; do not brown. Add the stock, herbes de Provence, garlic and barley and bring to a boil. Reduce the heat to low and simmer, uncovered, until the vegetables are tender when pierced with a fork, about 30 minutes. Add the potatoes, cover and cook over medium heat until tender, about 30 minutes.

Add the snap peas and mushrooms and cook for 5 minutes. Season to taste with salt and pepper. Transfer to a round 3-qt (3-l) baking dish 7–8 inches (18–20 cm) in diameter.

Preheat an oven to 400°F (200°C). To make the biscuits, in a bowl, sift together the flour, salt and baking powder. Using your fingers, rub the butter into the flour until it resembles coarse meal. Add the buttermilk and stir until the mixture forms a dough. Gather into a ball and transfer to a well-floured work surface. Roll out into a round about ¾ inch (2 cm) thick. Fold in half and roll out again. Fold one more time and roll out about ½ inch (12 mm) thick. Using a round cutter 2 inches (5 cm) in diameter, cut out 12 biscuits. Arrange them on top of the stew.

Bake until the biscuits are golden and the stew is bubbling, 20–25 minutes. Serve immediately.

Serves 6

Polenta Triangles with Saffron Tomatoes

FOR THE POLENTA:

6 cups (48 fl oz/1.5 l) water
1 teaspoon salt, plus salt to taste
1¼ cups (7½ oz/235 g) polenta or
 coarse-grind cornmeal
⅓ cup (1½ oz/45 g) freshly grated
 Parmesan cheese
2 teaspoons chopped fresh rosemary
freshly ground pepper

FOR THE SAUCE:

2 tablespoons olive oil
1 large yellow onion, chopped
¼ cup (2 fl oz/60 ml) dry red wine
1 tablespoon balsamic vinegar
⅛ teaspoon red pepper flakes
1 tablespoon tomato paste
¼ teaspoon dried oregano
4 cups (28 oz/875 g) peeled, seeded
 and finely chopped plum (Roma)
 tomatoes (fresh or canned)
salt and freshly ground pepper
1 teaspoon saffron threads

canola oil for deep-frying
2 cups (10 oz/315 g) all-purpose
 (plain) flour
½ cup (2 oz/60 g) freshly grated
 Parmesan cheese
fresh rosemary sprigs, optional

To make the polenta, butter a 9-inch (23-cm) square pan and set aside. In a large saucepan, bring the water to a boil. Add the 1 teaspoon salt and slowly stir in the polenta. Cook over medium heat, stirring, until the polenta pulls away from the sides of the pan, 20–30 minutes. Stir in the Parmesan, rosemary and salt and pepper to taste. Pour the polenta into the prepared pan and smooth the top. Cover and refrigerate to cool completely.

Meanwhile, make the sauce: In a large frying pan over medium heat, warm the olive oil. Add the onion and sauté, stirring, for 10 minutes. Stir in the red wine, vinegar, red pepper flakes, tomato paste, oregano, tomatoes and salt and pepper to taste. Reduce the heat to low and simmer, uncovered, until the sauce begins to thicken, about 20 minutes. Add the saffron and simmer for 5 minutes longer.

Remove the sauce from the heat and let cool slightly. Using a blender or a food processor fitted with the metal blade, purée the sauce until smooth. Transfer to a saucepan and keep warm.

Pour canola oil to a depth of ½ inch (12 mm) in a large, deep frying pan and heat until it registers 400°F (200°C) on a deep-fat frying thermometer.

Cut the polenta into nine 3-inch (7.5-cm) squares. Cut each square into 2 triangles; remove from the pan. Place the flour in a shallow bowl and, working with a few triangles at a time, toss in the flour to dust lightly. Slip the triangles into the hot oil a few at a time and fry, turning once, until golden brown, 4–6 minutes. Using a slotted spoon, transfer to paper towels to drain briefly.

To serve, arrange the triangles on a platter or individual plates. Spoon the tomato sauce over the polenta and sprinkle with the cheese. Garnish with rosemary sprigs, if desired, and serve.

Makes 18 triangles; serves 6

Black Beans and Rice with Corn Salsa

2 cups (14 oz/440 g) dried black beans
1 large yellow onion, chopped
1 large green bell pepper (capsicum), seeded, deribbed and cut into ½-inch (12-mm) dice

FOR THE CORN SALSA:
2 cups (12 oz/375 g) fresh corn kernels (from about 3 ears)
2 fresh jalapeño chili peppers, seeded and minced
2 tablespoons fresh lime juice
½ cup (2½ oz/75 g) finely chopped red (Spanish) onion
⅓ cup (½ oz/15 g) chopped fresh cilantro (fresh coriander)
salt and freshly ground pepper

¼ cup (2 fl oz/60 ml) olive oil
6 cloves garlic, finely chopped
⅓ cup (½ oz/15 g) chopped fresh parsley
¾ cup (1 oz/30 g) chopped fresh cilantro (fresh coriander)
1 tablespoon brown sugar
1 tablespoon ground cumin
1½ teaspoons dried oregano
2 teaspoons salt, plus salt to taste
freshly ground pepper
2 cups (16 fl oz/500 ml) water
1 cup (7 oz/220 g) basmati rice, rinsed and drained
¾ cup (6 fl oz/180 ml) dry white wine

Pick over the black beans and discard any misshapen beans or stones. Rinse the beans and drain. Place in a bowl, add plenty of water to cover and let soak for 3 hours.

Drain the beans and place in a saucepan with the yellow onion, bell pepper and water to cover by 2 inches (5 cm). Bring to a boil over high heat. Reduce the heat to medium-low and simmer, uncovered, until the beans are tender, about 1 hour. Remove from the heat and reserve the beans in their cooking liquid.

While the beans are cooking, make the salsa: Fill a saucepan three-fourths full with water and bring to a boil. Add the corn kernels and boil for 30 seconds. Drain, place in a bowl and let cool. Add the chili peppers, lime juice, red onion, cilantro and salt and ground pepper to taste. Mix well and set aside.

In a large frying pan over medium-low heat, warm the olive oil. Add the garlic, parsley, cilantro, brown sugar, cumin, oregano, 1½ teaspoons of the salt, and ground pepper to taste. Sauté, stirring occasionally, until the garlic is golden, about 10 minutes.

In a heavy saucepan, bring the water and the remaining ½ teaspoon salt to a boil. Add the rice, stir once, then cover, reduce the heat to low and cook for 20 minutes. After 20 minutes, uncover and check to see if the rice is tender and the water is absorbed. If not, re-cover and cook for a few minutes longer.

Meanwhile, add the white wine to the garlic mixture and simmer over high heat until the wine is reduced by one-fourth, about 5 minutes. Reduce the heat to medium, add the beans and their cooking liquid and simmer, uncovered, until the liquid has evaporated, about 15 minutes.

Spoon the rice into individual bowls. Top with the beans and the salsa. Serve at once.

Serves 6

Green and White Lasagne

½ lb (250 g) dried lasagne noodles
1 tub (15 oz/470 g) ricotta cheese
⅓ cup (1½ oz/45 g) freshly grated
   Parmesan cheese
salt and freshly ground pepper
¼ cup (2 fl oz/60 ml) extra-virgin
   olive oil
2 yellow onions, thinly sliced
4 zucchini (courgettes), about 1 lb
   (500 g) total weight, trimmed and
   thinly sliced crosswise
1 lb (500 g) fresh mushrooms, brushed
   clean and thinly sliced
3 cloves garlic, minced
¼ cup (2 oz/60 g) unsalted butter
¼ cup (1½ oz/45 g) all-purpose
   (plain) flour
3 cups (24 fl oz/750 ml) milk
freshly grated nutmeg
40 fresh basil leaves
½ lb (250 g) whole-milk mozzarella,
   shredded

*F*ill a large pot three-fourths full with water, salt it lightly, and bring to a boil over high heat. Add the lasagne noodles and cook until *al dente,* 10–12 minutes or according to package directions. Meanwhile, fill a large bowl with cold water. When the pasta is done, drain and place in the bowl of water to cool. After 5 minutes, drain the pasta again and lay the pieces in a single layer on a baking sheet. Cover with plastic wrap and set aside.

In a small bowl, stir together the ricotta, Parmesan and salt and pepper to taste until well mixed. Set aside.

In a large frying pan over medium heat, warm the olive oil. Add the onions and cook, stirring occasionally, until soft, about 10 minutes. Add the zucchini, mushrooms and garlic and continue to cook, stirring occasionally, until the vegetables are tender and any moisture has evaporated, 10–12 minutes. Season to taste with salt and pepper. Set aside.

In a saucepan over low heat, melt the butter. Whisk in the flour and cook, stirring, for 2 minutes. Gradually whisk in the milk and cook, stirring, until the sauce is smooth and thickened, 3–4 minutes. Season to taste with salt, pepper and nutmeg.

Position a rack in the upper third of an oven and preheat to 375°F (190°C). Oil a 9-by-13-inch (23-by-33-cm) baking dish.

Cover the bottom of the prepared baking dish with a layer of lasagne noodles. Spoon one-third of the ricotta mixture over the noodles. Sprinkle one-third of the reserved vegetables over the ricotta layer and then top evenly with one-third of the white sauce. Distribute about one-third of the basil leaves evenly over the sauce. Repeat the layers twice more, ending with the basil. Sprinkle the mozzarella evenly over the top.

Bake until golden and bubbling around the edges, 30–40 minutes. Let cool briefly, then cut into squares to serve.

Serves 8–10

Tostada Salad with Tomatillo Salsa

1 cup (7 oz/220 g) dried black beans

FOR THE TOMATILLO SALSA:
2 cans (12 oz/375 g each) tomatillos, drained and chopped
⅓ cup (½ oz/15 g) lightly packed, chopped fresh cilantro (fresh coriander)
¼ cup (1½ oz/45 g) minced red (Spanish) onion
2 tablespoons fresh lime juice
½ fresh jalapeño or serrano chili pepper, seeded and minced
salt and freshly ground pepper

1 cup (8 fl oz/250 ml) corn oil
6 corn tortillas, each 6 inches (15 cm) in diameter
2 cups (8 oz/250 g) coarsely shredded Monterey jack cheese
1 small head romaine (cos) lettuce, carefully washed, well dried and thinly sliced crosswise

Garnish this popular Mexican-style salad with sour cream, chopped green (spring) onions, sliced avocados, lime wedges and cilantro sprigs, if you like. Other cheeses, such as sharp Cheddar or mozzarella, can be used in place of the jack cheese.

❧

Pick over the black beans and discard any misshapen beans or stones. Rinse the beans and drain. Place in a bowl, add plenty of water to cover and let soak for 3 hours.

Drain the beans and place in a saucepan with water to cover by 2 inches (5 cm). Bring to a boil over high heat. Reduce the heat to low and simmer, uncovered, until the beans are tender, about 1 hour. Remove from the heat and drain. Set aside.

To make the salsa, in a bowl, stir together the tomatillos, cilantro, onion, lime juice, chili pepper and salt and pepper to taste. Set aside.

In a frying pan over medium-high heat, warm the corn oil. When it is hot, slip a tortilla into the oil and cook until golden and almost crisp, 1–2 minutes. Using tongs, transfer to paper towels to drain. Repeat with the remaining tortillas.

To serve, place each tortilla on a plate. Distribute the beans, cheese, lettuce and salsa evenly over the tortillas.

Serves 6

Roasted Pepper Frittata

1 red bell pepper (capsicum)
1 yellow bell pepper (capsicum)
1 green bell pepper (capsicum)
2 cloves garlic, minced
2 teaspoons balsamic vinegar
¼ teaspoon dried oregano
salt and freshly ground pepper
8 eggs
3 tablespoons milk
½ cup (2 oz/60 g) freshly grated
  Parmesan cheese
1½ tablespoons olive oil

Although a frittata, or Italian-style flat omelet, is commonly served as a first course, here it is offered as a colorful and satisfying main dish. Garnish the frittata with bell pepper slices and flat-leaf (Italian) parsley sprigs, if you wish.

❧

Preheat a broiler (griller).

Cut all the bell peppers in half lengthwise and remove the stems, seeds and ribs. Place cut sides down on a baking sheet. Broil (grill) until the skins blacken and blister (see page 10). Remove the baking sheet from the broiler, drape the peppers loosely with aluminum foil and let cool for 10 minutes. Using your fingers or a small knife, remove the pepper skins. Cut the peppers lengthwise into strips ¼ inch (6 mm) wide.

In a bowl, combine the bell pepper strips, garlic, vinegar, oregano and salt and pepper to taste. Let marinate for 30 minutes.

In another bowl, whisk together the eggs, milk and Parmesan cheese until frothy. Add the pepper mixture and mix well. Season to taste with salt and pepper.

Preheat an oven to 400°F (200°C).

In a 10-inch (25-cm) nonstick ovenproof frying pan over medium-high heat, warm the olive oil. When the oil is hot, add the egg mixture and, when it starts to set, lift the edges of the frittata with a spatula so that some of the egg mixture runs underneath. Reduce the heat to medium and cook until the bottom is set but the top is still runny, 8–10 minutes. Place the pan in the oven and cook until the eggs are set on top and golden brown on the bottom, 6–7 minutes.

Remove the frittata from the oven and loosen with a spatula. Invert the frittata onto a serving plate. Cut into wedges and serve hot or at room temperature.

Serves 6

Hummus Pita Sandwiches

⅔ cup (4½ oz/140 g) dried chick-peas (garbanzo beans) or 1¼ cups (8 oz/ 250 g) canned chick-peas

juice of 1 lemon, plus fresh lemon juice to taste

¼ cup (2½ oz/75 g) tahini

2 tablespoons olive oil

1 tablespoon water

3 cloves garlic, minced

¼ teaspoon ground cumin

salt

3 pita breads, warmed

6 lettuce leaves, such as butter or romaine (cos), carefully washed and well dried

2 tomatoes, cut into ½-inch (12-mm) dice

½ small red (Spanish) onion, cut into ½-inch (12-mm) dice

12 Kalamata olives, pitted and coarsely chopped

Hummus is a Middle Eastern purée made from chick-peas, lemon juice, olive oil, garlic and the ground sesame paste known as tahini. It is often served as a first-course spread for pita bread and, here, embellishes a sandwich of lettuce, tomatoes, red onions and black olives.

❧

*I*f using dried chick-peas, pick them over and discard any misshapen peas or stones. Rinse the chick-peas and drain. Place in a bowl, add plenty of water to cover and let soak for 3 hours.

Drain the chick-peas and place in a saucepan with water to cover by 2 inches (5 cm). Bring to a boil over high heat. Reduce the heat to low and simmer, uncovered, until tender, 50–60 minutes. Remove from the heat and drain, reserving the cooking liquid.

If using canned chick-peas, drain them, reserving the canning liquid, and set aside.

In a food processor fitted with the metal blade or in a blender, combine the chick-peas, the juice of 1 lemon, tahini, olive oil, water, garlic, cumin and ½ cup (4 fl oz/ 125 ml) of the reserved cooking or canning liquid; discard the remaining cooking or canning liquid. Process until a soft and creamy paste forms. Season to taste with salt and additional lemon juice.

Cut the pita breads in half to form 6 pockets. Spread an equal amount of the hummus inside each pocket. Then tuck a lettuce leaf and an equal amount of the tomato, red onion and olives in each pocket.

Arrange the sandwiches on a platter and serve.

Serves 6

Lemon, Sesame, and Garlic Hummus

MAKES ABOUT 3 1/2 CUPS

For anyone who doesn't like to eat meat every day, legumes are a great source of plant protein. Serve this hummus with rice crackers or fresh veggie slices for a healthy snack. For a light lunch, stuff in pita bread with baby spinach leaves. For a zesty, enticing dip, puree guacamole into the mixture.

- 1–3 cloves garlic, peeled and crushed
- 2 tablespoons olive oil
- 2 tablespoons white sesame seeds, toasted
- 2 tablespoons tahini
- 2 tablespoons lemon juice
- 1 (15-ounce) can garbanzo beans, drained, liquid reserved
- salt and white pepper to taste
- 1 tablespoon orange peel, minced
- 1 1/2 tablespoons lemon peel, minced

In a blender or food processor, combine garlic, olive oil, sesame seeds, tahini, lemon juice, and garbanzo beans (reserve about a tablespoon of beans for garnish).

Blend, adding reserved garbanzo-bean liquid if needed until hummus reaches desired consistency. Season with salt and pepper.

Transfer the mixture to a medium serving bowl. Garnish in the middle with reserved garbanzo beans. Sprinkle orange and lemon peel around the beans. Chill in the refrigerator, tightly covered, until ready to serve.

Per 1/4 cup: 75 calories; 2 g protein; 4 g fat; 8 g carb; 2 g fiber.

Ricotta and Spinach Dumplings with Pesto

3 lb (1.5 kg) spinach, stemmed, carefully washed and well dried

1 tablespoon water

1 cup (4 oz/120 g) freshly grated or shredded Parmesan cheese

1 cup (5 oz/150 g) all-purpose (plain) flour, plus flour as needed

1½ cups (12 oz/375 g) ricotta cheese

3 eggs, lightly beaten

large pinch of freshly grated nutmeg

salt and freshly ground pepper

3 tablespoons extra-virgin olive oil

1¼ cups (10 fl oz/310 ml) pesto
    (recipe on page 12)

This dish can also be served with tomato sauce in place of the pesto. Garnish with fresh basil sprigs or orange zest curls.

In a large frying pan over high heat, combine the spinach and water. Cook, using tongs to gently toss the spinach, until it wilts, about 2 minutes. Transfer to a colander and press out the excess water with the back of a large spoon. Wrap the spinach in a clean kitchen towel or paper towels and wring out any excess moisture. Transfer to a cutting board and chop finely.

In a bowl, combine the chopped spinach, ½ cup (2 oz/60 g) of the Parmesan, ½ cup (2½ oz/75 g) of the flour, the ricotta and eggs. Season to taste with the nutmeg, salt and pepper and stir well. Spread another ½ cup (2½ oz/75 g) of the flour on a plate. Using a spoon, shape the dough into walnut-sized oval dumplings and, working with 2 or 3 at a time, dredge them in the flour. If the dough is too wet and will not form a ball, add more flour, 1 tablespoon at a time, until it holds a shape.

Preheat an oven to 350°F (180°C).

Fill a large pot three-fourths full with water, salt it lightly, and bring to a boil. Add the dumplings, a few at a time, and boil until they rise to the surface, 5–7 minutes. Using a slotted spoon, transfer the dumplings to an oiled 2-qt (2-l) baking dish. Drizzle with the olive oil and toss gently to coat.

Bake until the dumplings are hot, 10–15 minutes.

To serve, spoon the pesto sauce onto a warmed platter or individual plates and arrange the dumplings on top. Sprinkle with the remaining ½ cup (2 oz/60 g) Parmesan cheese. Serve at once.

Makes about 36 dumplings; serves 6

Caramelized Onion and Cheddar Soufflé

3 tablespoons vegetable oil

3 yellow onions, 1¼ lb (625 g) total
  weight, thinly sliced

½ teaspoon chopped fresh thyme

salt and freshly ground pepper

1 cup (8 fl oz/250 ml) milk

1 cup (8 fl oz/250 ml) half-and-half
  (half cream)

5 tablespoons (2½ oz/75 g) unsalted
  butter

5 tablespoons (1½ oz/45 g) all-purpose
  (plain) flour

6 eggs, separated

1¼ cups (5 oz/155 g) coarsely shredded
  Cheddar cheese

¼ cup (1 oz/30 g) freshly grated
  Parmesan cheese

*Make sure your guests are seated and waiting for the soufflé
when it is removed from the oven, as it will sink quickly.*

In a frying pan over medium-low heat, warm the oil. Add
the onions and thyme, cover and cook, stirring occasionally,
until very soft, about 20 minutes. Uncover and continue to
cook, stirring occasionally, until lightly golden, about 30
minutes longer. Season to taste with salt and pepper. Transfer the onions to a sieve set over a bowl; set aside to drain.

Position a rack in the lower third of an oven and preheat
to 350°F (180°C). Butter a 2-qt (2-l) soufflé dish.

In a saucepan over medium-high heat, combine the milk
and half-and-half and bring to a boil. Meanwhile, in another
saucepan over low heat, melt the butter. Whisk the flour
into the butter. Cook, whisking constantly, for 2 minutes.
Slowly pour the hot milk mixture into the butter mixture,
whisking vigorously. Cook, stirring, until thick and smooth,
2–3 minutes. Transfer to a bowl and let cool for 10 minutes.

Add the drained onions and mix well. Stir in the egg
yolks, one at a time. Add the Cheddar cheese and mix well.
Season to taste with salt and pepper.

In a clean bowl, beat the egg whites until stiff peaks form.
Fold half of the egg whites into the cheese-mixture base.
Then fold in the remaining egg whites just until combined;
do not overmix. Pour the mixture into the prepared soufflé
dish and sprinkle with the Parmesan cheese. Bake until
well browned and firmly set when gently shaken, 40–50
minutes. Serve immediately.

Serves 6–8

Stir-fried Tofu, Green Beans and Cashews

¼ cup (2 fl oz/60 ml) soy sauce

3 tablespoons dry sherry

2 teaspoons cornstarch (cornflour)

1 package (14 oz/440 g) firm tofu, well drained and cut into ½-inch (12-mm) dice

½ cup (2½ oz/75 g) raw cashews

1 lb (500 g) green beans, trimmed and halved on the diagonal

3 tablespoons vegetable oil

6 unpeeled fresh ginger slices (¼ inch/ 6 mm thick)

2 red (Spanish) onions, cut into ½-inch (12-mm) dice

1 cup (8 fl oz/250 ml) vegetable stock *(recipe on page 12)*

½ teaspoon hot chili oil

Tofu, the popular Asian curd made from soybeans, is beneficial to any diet, as it is low in calories and high in protein. Water-packed cubes of tofu can be found in the refrigerator case of most well-stocked markets.

☙

*P*reheat an oven to 350°F (180°C). In a large bowl, whisk together the soy sauce, sherry and cornstarch until the cornstarch is dissolved. Add the tofu and stir gently to coat. Set aside.

Spread the cashews on a baking sheet and bake until golden, 12–15 minutes. Remove from the oven and set aside.

Fill a large saucepan three-fourths full with water, salt it lightly, and bring to a boil. Add the green beans and cook until almost tender, about 3 minutes. Drain and set aside.

In a wok or large, deep frying pan over high heat, warm 2 tablespoons of the vegetable oil. When the oil is hot, add the ginger and, using a wok spatula or wooden spoon, stir and toss until fragrant, about 1 minute. Remove the ginger and discard.

Using the spatula or spoon, remove the tofu from the marinade, reserving the marinade. Add the tofu to the pan. Stir and toss over high heat until the tofu is hot and golden on the outside, about 3 minutes. Transfer the tofu to a clean bowl and set aside.

Reduce the heat to medium. Add the remaining 1 tablespoon oil to the pan. Add the onions and stir and toss until almost wilted, 5–7 minutes. Raise the heat to high and return the tofu to the pan, along with the green beans, reserved marinade, stock and hot chili oil. Stirring constantly, bring the mixture to a boil. Boil, stirring, for about 30 seconds until the mixture thickens.

Remove from the heat and stir in the cashews. Transfer to a serving dish and serve immediately.

Serves 6

Corn-and-Jalapeño Pancakes with Tomato Salsa

2 cups (12 oz/375 g) fresh corn kernels (cut from about 3 ears or frozen)

5 fresh jalapeño chili peppers, seeded and minced

2 cloves garlic, finely chopped

l red bell pepper (capsicum), seeded, deribbed and finely diced

6 green (spring) onions, white part and 2 inches (5 cm) of the tender green tops, thinly sliced

2 eggs

1¼ cups (6½ oz/200 g) all-purpose (plain) flour

½ cup (2½ oz/75 g) cornmeal

1 teaspoon baking powder

1 teaspoon salt, plus salt to taste

2 tablespoons fresh lime juice

1½ cups (12 fl oz/375 ml) milk

freshly ground pepper

FOR THE TOMATO SALSA:

1½ cups (9 oz/280 g) diced tomatoes

¼ cup (1½ oz/45 g) finely chopped red (Spanish) onion

1 fresh jalapeño or serrano chili pepper, seeded and minced

2 tablespoons fresh lime juice

5 tablespoons chopped fresh cilantro (fresh coriander)

salt and freshly ground pepper

about ⅓ cup (3 fl oz/80 ml) vegetable oil

1¼ cups (10 fl oz/310 ml) sour cream

Studded with corn and embellished with chilies and bell peppers, these zesty pancakes are as delicious as they are colorful. Serve them as a light meal at any time of the day—from breakfast to dinner.

※

*F*ill a saucepan three-fourths full with water, salt it lightly, and bring to a boil. Add the corn kernels and cook for 1 minute. Drain, place in a large bowl and let cool. Add the chili peppers, garlic, bell pepper and green onions, mix well and set aside.

In a food processor fitted with the metal blade, combine the eggs, flour, cornmeal, baking powder, 1 teaspoon salt and the lime juice. Pulse a few times to mix. Add the milk and pulse a few more times to form a smooth batter. Add to the corn mixture and stir to mix. Season to taste with more salt, if needed, and pepper. Let stand at room temperature for 30 minutes.

To make the tomato salsa, in a bowl, stir together the tomatoes, red onion, chili pepper, lime juice, cilantro and salt and pepper to taste. Set aside.

In a large frying pan over medium heat, warm 2 tablespoons of the oil. Working in batches, spoon the batter into the pan to form pancakes 3 inches (7.5 cm) in diameter; do not crowd the pan. Cook, turning once, until golden brown on both sides, 5–6 minutes total. Using a slotted spatula, transfer to paper towels to drain. Repeat with the remaining batter, adding oil as needed to prevent sticking.

Place the pancakes on a platter or individual plates and top with the sour cream and salsa. Serve at once.

Makes about 24 pancakes; serves 6

Couscous with Winter Vegetable Stew

2 tablespoons unsalted butter
1 teaspoon saffron threads
1 teaspoon ground cumin
2 cinnamon sticks, each about 3 inches (7.5 cm) long
½ teaspoon ground turmeric
3 yellow onions, quartered
2 cloves garlic, chopped
½ fresh jalapeño chili pepper, seeded
1 small bunch fresh cilantro (fresh coriander), tied together
3 tomatoes, peeled, seeded (*see page 11*) and quartered
6 cups (48 fl oz/1.5 l) vegetable stock (*recipe on page 12*)
3 carrots, peeled and cut into 1-inch (2.5-cm) lengths
3 small turnips, peeled and quartered
1 lb (500 g) butternut (pumpkin) squash, peeled, halved and seeded
3 small zucchini (courgettes), trimmed
salt to taste, plus ½ teaspoon salt
freshly ground pepper
1¾ cups (14 fl oz/440 ml) water
1¾ cups (10½ oz/330 g) couscous

FOR THE HARISSA SAUCE:
1 cup (8 fl oz/250 ml) broth from stew
2 teaspoons harissa
1 tablespoon fresh lemon juice
1 tablespoon chopped fresh cilantro (fresh coriander)
salt and freshly ground pepper

To make the sauce for this fragrant stew, look for harissa, a spicy red pepper condiment from North Africa sold in specialty-food stores. Garnish with chopped fresh cilantro and parsley.

❧

*I*n a large soup pot over medium heat, melt the butter. Add the saffron, cumin, cinnamon sticks, turmeric, onions, garlic, chili pepper, cilantro and tomatoes. Stir until well mixed. Cover and simmer for 5 minutes. Add the vegetable stock, re-cover and simmer for another 30 minutes to meld the flavors. Add the carrots and turnips, re-cover and continue to simmer until tender when pierced with a fork, about 30 minutes longer.

Cut the butternut squash and zucchini into 1-inch (2.5-cm) chunks and add them to the stew. Cover and simmer until tender when pressed with a fork, about 20 minutes. Season to taste with salt and pepper. Discard the cinnamon sticks, chili pepper and cilantro bundle.

About 10 minutes before the stew is ready, in a saucepan, bring the water to a boil. Remove from the heat and stir in the couscous and ½ teaspoon salt. Cover and let stand for 10 minutes.

To make the harissa sauce, in a bowl, stir together the broth, harissa, lemon juice, cilantro and salt and pepper to taste.

Uncover the couscous and fluff with a fork. Spread the couscous on a large platter and make a well in the center. Using a slotted spoon, place the vegetables in the well. Moisten the couscous with a few spoonfuls of the broth. Serve with the harissa sauce and the remaining broth in separate bowls on the side.

Serves 6–8

Leek and Goat Cheese Tart

FOR THE PASTRY:

1 cup (5 oz/155 g) all-purpose (plain) flour, plus extra for dusting

¼ teaspoon salt

½ cup (4 oz/125 g) unsalted butter, cut into 1-inch (2.5-cm) pieces

2–4 tablespoons water

FOR THE FILLING:

2 tablespoons unsalted butter

3 leeks, white part and 2 inches (5 cm) of the green, halved lengthwise, carefully washed, well dried and cut into ¾-inch (2-cm) dice

salt and freshly ground pepper

¼ lb (125 g) fresh goat cheese

¼ cup (1 oz/30 g) freshly grated Parmesan cheese

¾ cup (6 fl oz/180 ml) half-and-half (half cream)

3 eggs

To make the pastry, in a bowl, mix together the flour and salt. Add the butter and, using an electric mixer fitted with the paddle attachment on low speed or your fingers, beat or rub in the butter until it resembles coarse meal. Sprinkle in the water, a little at a time, and beat just until the mixture holds together.

Gather the dough into a ball and flatten into a 6-inch (15-cm) round. Wrap in plastic wrap; chill in the refrigerator for 1 hour.

Meanwhile, to begin making the filling, in a large frying pan over medium-low heat, melt the butter. Add the leeks and cook, stirring occasionally, until soft and no moisture remains in the pan, about 30 minutes. Season to taste with salt and pepper. Transfer to a bowl and let cool.

On a well-floured work surface, roll out the pastry into a round 10 inches (25 cm) in diameter. Drape the pastry over the rolling pin and carefully transfer it to a 9-inch (23-cm) tart pan with a removable bottom. Press the pastry firmly but gently into the pan. Trim the edges even with the rim. Freeze the pastry shell until firm, about 20 minutes.

Meanwhile, preheat an oven to 325°F (165°C).

Line the pastry shell with aluminum foil and fill with dried beans. Bake until the pastry turns golden on the edges, about 15 minutes. Remove the beans and foil and continue to bake until lightly golden, 3–5 minutes longer.

Meanwhile, finish making the filling: Crumble the goat cheese into a bowl. Add the Parmesan, half-and-half, eggs and salt and pepper to taste and whisk until blended. Stir in the leeks.

Pour the filling into the warm prebaked tart shell. Bake until set and a thin skewer inserted into the center comes out clean, 20–30 minutes.

Let cool for 5 minutes, then cut into wedges to serve.

Serves 6–8

Vegetable Curry with Brown Rice

1 cup (7 oz/220 g) short- or long-grain
  brown rice

3 cups (24 fl oz/750 ml) water

½ teaspoon salt

3 tablespoons unsalted butter

2 yellow onions, quartered

2 celery stalks, finely diced

2 carrots, peeled and cut into slices
  ½ inch (12 mm) thick

1 fresh jalapeño or serrano chili pepper,
  seeded and minced

4 cloves garlic, minced

2 tablespoons all-purpose (plain) flour

6 small red potatoes, ¾ lb (375 g) total
  weight, unpeeled and well scrubbed

3 cups (24 fl oz/750 ml) vegetable stock
  (recipe on page 12)

3 tablespoons curry powder

2 tablespoons peeled and minced or
  grated fresh ginger

¼ cup (2 fl oz/60 ml) canned coconut
  milk or heavy (double) cream

3 cups (12 oz/375 g) cauliflower florets

3 cups (12 oz/375 g) broccoli florets

Serve this substantial curry dish with a range of savory garnishes like toasted almonds or peanuts, toasted or fresh shaved coconut, sliced bananas, dried currants, raisins, chopped green (spring) onions and chutney. Arrange the garnishes in separate small bowls at the table, if you like, and allow your guests to help themselves.

Rinse the rice in several changes of water and drain. In a heavy saucepan over high heat, combine the water and salt and bring to a boil over high heat. Add the rice, stir once or twice, and reduce the heat to low. Cover and cook, without stirring, for 45 minutes; do not remove the cover.

Meanwhile, in a large soup pot over medium-high heat, melt the butter. Add the onions, celery and carrots and cook, stirring occasionally, until the onions are soft, about 10 minutes. Reduce the heat to medium, add the chili pepper and garlic and cook, stirring, for 2 minutes to blend the flavors. Sprinkle the flour over the vegetables and continue to cook, stirring, for 2 minutes longer.

Cut the potatoes in half. Add them to the vegetables along with the stock, curry powder, ginger and coconut milk or cream. Cover and simmer gently, stirring occasionally, for 15 minutes. Add the cauliflower and broccoli and continue to simmer, stirring occasionally, until the vegetables are tender when pierced with a fork, about 20 minutes longer.

After the rice has cooked for 45 minutes, uncover and check if it is tender and the water is absorbed. If not, re-cover and cook for a few minutes longer.

Spoon the rice onto a large platter or individual plates. Make a well in the center and spoon the curry into the well. Serve immediately.

Serves 6

Polenta with Vegetable Ragout

7 cups (56 fl oz/1.75 l) water

1 teaspoon salt, plus salt to taste

1¾ cups (10½ oz/330 g) polenta or
  coarse-grind cornmeal

freshly ground pepper

2 tablespoons extra-virgin olive oil

1 small yellow onion, chopped

1 small celery stalk, chopped

1 small carrot, peeled and chopped

1 clove garlic, minced

2 teaspoons chopped fresh sage

½ teaspoon chopped fresh thyme

1 teaspoon chopped fresh rosemary

4 cups (28 oz/875 g) peeled, seeded
  and finely chopped tomatoes (fresh
  or canned)

5 tablespoons (2½ oz/75 g) unsalted
  butter

¼ cup (1½ oz/45 g) all-purpose (plain)
  flour

3 cups (24 fl oz/750 ml) milk

large pinch of freshly grated nutmeg

1 cup (4 oz/125 g) freshly grated
  Parmesan cheese

*I*n a large, heavy saucepan over high heat, bring the water to a boil. Add the 1 teaspoon salt and then slowly pour in the polenta, stirring constantly. Reduce the heat to medium and cook, stirring, until the polenta pulls away from the sides of the pan, 20–30 minutes. Season to taste with salt and pepper. Turn out onto a smooth work surface and, using a rubber spatula, spread it evenly to form a sheet ½ inch (12 mm) thick. Let cool completely.

In a large sauté pan over medium-low heat, warm the oil. Add the onion, celery, carrot, garlic, sage, thyme and rosemary. Cook, stirring occasionally, until the onion is soft, about 15 minutes. Add the tomatoes and any juices and simmer, stirring occasionally, until thick, 20–25 minutes. Remove from the heat.

Using a round cutter 2½ inches (6 cm) in diameter, cut out as many rounds as possible from the polenta sheet. Arrange half of the polenta rounds in a single layer on the bottom of a 9-by-13-inch (23-by-33-cm) baking dish.

Preheat an oven to 350°F (180°C).

In a saucepan over low heat, melt the butter. Whisk in the flour and cook, whisking constantly, for 2 minutes; do not brown. Slowly add the milk, whisking constantly. Continue to whisk until smooth and thickened, 3–4 minutes. Season to taste with salt and pepper and the nutmeg. Remove from the heat.

Spoon half of the white sauce evenly over the polenta rounds. Spread with half of the tomato sauce. Repeat layering with the remaining polenta, white sauce and tomato sauce. Sprinkle with the Parmesan cheese.

Bake until golden on top and bubbling around the edges, about 20 minutes. Let cool for 10 minutes, then spoon onto warmed plates.

Serves 6

Falafel Burgers with Tahini Mayonnaise

2 cups (10 oz/315 g) dry falafel mix
1⅓ cups (11 fl oz/330 ml) cold water
½ cup (4 fl oz/125 ml) garlic mayonnaise
  (recipe on page 13)
1 tablespoon tahini
1 teaspoon ground cumin
2 teaspoons warm water
salt and freshly ground pepper
canola oil for deep-frying
6 crusty round rolls, each 2½ inches
  (6 cm) in diameter, halved
6 romaine (cos) lettuce leaves, carefully
  washed, well dried and cut crosswise
  into strips 1 inch (2.5 cm) wide
1 large tomato, cut into 6 thin slices

In Syria, Lebanon, Israel and Egypt, this is street food, but arguably some of the most nutritious and flavorful of its kind in the world. If you like, serve each burger with a slice of red (Spanish) onion.

❧

In a bowl, stir together the falafel mix and cold water. Let stand until the mixture thickens, about 30 minutes.

Meanwhile, place the mayonnaise in another bowl. Adding a little at a time, whisk in the tahini. When all of the tahini has been added, whisk in the cumin, warm water and salt and pepper to taste. Set aside.

In a deep saucepan, pour in canola oil to a depth of 1 inch (2.5 cm). Heat to 375°F (190°C) on a deep-fat frying thermometer, or until a small drop of the falafel mixture sizzles immediately upon contact with the oil. While the oil is heating, using your hands, form the falafel mixture into 6 patties, each 2½ inches (6 cm) in diameter and ½ inch (12 mm) thick.

Slip the patties into the hot oil a few at a time and fry, turning once, until golden on both sides, about 6 minutes total. Using tongs or a slotted spoon, transfer the patties to paper towels and keep them warm while you fry the remaining patties.

Place a falafel burger on the bottom of each roll. Top each burger with a spoonful of the tahini mayonnaise, some lettuce leaf strips and a tomato slice. Cap with the top of the roll and serve immediately.

Serves 6

Baked Penne with Three Cheeses

6 tablespoons (3 oz/90 g) unsalted butter

6 tablespoons (2 oz/60 g) all-purpose (plain) flour

4 cups (32 fl oz/1 l) milk

1½ cups (6 oz/185 g) shredded Fontina cheese

½ lb (250 g) Gorgonzola cheese, cut into pieces

1 cup (4 oz/125 g) freshly grated Parmesan cheese

salt and freshly ground pepper

¾ lb (375 g) dried penne pasta

½ cup (1 oz/30 g) fresh bread crumbs

Other short dried pastas—fusilli, farfalle, elbow macaroni, shells—can be used in place of the penne. This recipe can also be made in individual 5-inch (13-cm) round gratin dishes, in which case the baking time should be reduced by 5–10 minutes.

☙

*I*n a large saucepan over medium heat, melt the butter. Whisk in the flour and cook, stirring constantly, for 2 minutes; do not brown. Gradually whisk in the milk and cook, stirring constantly, until the sauce is smooth and thickened, about 5 minutes. Add the Fontina, Gorgonzola and Parmesan and stir until the cheeses melt. Season to taste with salt and pepper. Remove from the heat; set aside.

Preheat an oven to 375°F (190°C). Oil a shallow 2½-qt (2.5-l) baking dish.

Fill a large pot three-fourths full with water, salt it lightly, and bring to a boil over high heat. Add the pasta and cook until *al dente,* 10–12 minutes or according to package directions. Drain and add to the sauce. Toss gently to mix.

Transfer the pasta and sauce to the prepared dish. Sprinkle the top evenly with the bread crumbs. Bake until the top is golden and the sauce is bubbling, 25–30 minutes.

Let cool for 5 minutes, then spoon into warmed bowls and serve.

Serves 6

Made ½ recipe
Used rice flour pasta
delicious

Asian Turnovers

1 tablespoon Asian sesame oil

1 tablespoon peanut oil

½ lb (250 g) Chinese or Savoy cabbage
  leaves, cut into ½-inch (12-mm)
  pieces

½ lb (250 g) sugar snap peas, trimmed
  and halved on the diagonal

½ lb (250 g) fresh mushrooms, brushed
  clean and thinly sliced

6 green (spring) onions, thinly sliced

2 tablespoons peeled and minced fresh
  ginger

1 tablespoon soy sauce

1 tablespoon dry sherry

salt and freshly ground pepper

all-purpose (plain) flour for dusting

1 box (17¼ oz/535 g) frozen puff pastry
  (2 sheets), thawed

2 egg yolks beaten with 2 tablespoons
  water

FOR THE DIPPING SAUCE:

½ cup (4 fl oz/125 ml) soy sauce

¼ cup (2 fl oz/60 ml) rice wine vinegar

½ teaspoon hot-pepper sauce

½ teaspoon sugar

½ cup (¾ oz/20 g) chopped fresh
  cilantro (fresh coriander)

You can also serve these tasty turnovers as a first course.

In a large frying pan or wok over medium-high heat, warm the sesame and peanut oils. When the oils are hot, add the cabbage and snap peas and cook, stirring constantly, until the cabbage wilts, 3–4 minutes. Increase the heat to high and add the mushrooms, green onions, ginger, soy sauce and sherry. Continue to cook, stirring constantly, until the mushrooms are soft and the mixture is dry, about 5 minutes. Transfer to a bowl and season to taste with salt and pepper. Let cool completely.

Preheat an oven to 400°F (200°C).

To assemble the turnovers, on a well-floured surface and using a floured rolling pin, roll out 1 puff pastry sheet about ⅛ inch (3 mm) thick. Using a round cutter 4 inches (10 cm) in diameter, cut out 8 rounds from the dough. Place about 2 tablespoons of the filling on one-half of a round. Brush the edges of the opposite half lightly with the egg-water mixture. Fold the round in half to enclose the filling; press the edges together firmly to seal. Repeat with the remaining rounds. Place the turnovers on an ungreased baking sheet, spacing them about 2 inches (5 cm) apart. Repeat with the remaining pastry sheet and filling. Brush the top side of each turnover with the remaining egg mixture.

Bake until golden, about 15 minutes.

Meanwhile, make the dipping sauce: In a bowl, stir together the soy sauce, vinegar, hot-pepper sauce, sugar and cilantro until the sugar dissolves and the ingredients are well mixed. Divide evenly among small individual sauce bowls.

Serve the turnovers hot from the oven, accompanied with the dipping sauce.

Makes 16 turnovers; serves 4–6

Pizza with Smoked Gouda, Spicy Peppers and Cilantro

2 tablespoons fresh lime juice

3 tablespoons extra-virgin olive oil

salt and freshly ground pepper

¾ lb (375 g) cherry tomatoes, halved

2 purchased 9-inch (23-cm) partially baked pizza crusts or ¾ lb (375 g) purchased pizza dough

all-purpose (plain) flour for dusting

6 oz (185 g) smoked Gouda cheese, coarsely shredded

½ red bell pepper (capsicum), seeded, deribbed and cut into long, very narrow strips

½ green bell pepper (capsicum), seeded, deribbed and cut into long, very narrow strips

1 fresh jalapeño or serrano chili pepper, seeded and minced

¼ cup (¼ oz/7 g) coarsely chopped fresh cilantro (fresh coriander) leaves

Any smoked cheese works well in this recipe, including smoked mozzarella, Cheddar or Monterey jack. To give this pizza an Italian accent, substitute an equal amount of basil and balsamic vinegar for the cilantro and lime juice. For a crisper crust, bake the pizza on a pizza stone placed on the lowest rack of an oven.

❧

*P*osition 2 oven racks near the center of an oven and preheat to 500°F (260°C).

In a bowl, whisk together the lime juice, olive oil and salt and pepper to taste. Add the tomatoes, turn to coat and set aside.

If using the pizza dough, divide the dough in half. On a well-floured work surface, roll out each half into a 9-inch (23-cm) round. The edges of the dough should be slightly thicker than the center.

Place each dough round or partially baked pizza crust on a heavy-duty baking sheet. Sprinkle half of the cheese evenly over each round to within ½ inch (12 mm) of the edge. Then top each round with half of the red and green bell peppers and half of the minced chili pepper.

Bake until the crusts are crisp and golden, 10–12 minutes; switch pan positions halfway through baking. Remove the pizzas from the oven and distribute half of the tomatoes and cilantro over each one.

Cut into wedges and serve immediately.

Makes two 9-inch (23-cm) pizzas; serves 6

Gratin of Zucchini, Eggplant and Chick-peas

½ cup (3½ oz/105 g) dried chick-peas
   (garbanzo beans)

3 tablespoons olive oil

2 small yellow onions, quartered

1 large green bell pepper (capsicum),
   seeded, deribbed and cut into 1-inch
   (2.5-cm) squares

3 slender (Asian) eggplants (aubergines),
   about ¾ lb (375 g) total weight, cut
   crosswise into slices 1 inch (2.5 cm)
   thick

3 zucchini (courgettes), about ¾ lb
   (375 g) total weight, cut crosswise
   into slices 1 inch (2.5 cm) thick

4 cloves garlic, finely chopped

1½ cups (9 oz/280 g) peeled, seeded and
   chopped tomatoes (fresh or canned)

1 cup (8 fl oz/250 ml) vegetable stock
   (recipe on page 12)

¼ teaspoon red pepper flakes

¼ cup (¼ oz/7 g) chopped fresh basil or
   2 tablespoons dried basil

1 teaspoon chopped fresh thyme or
   ½ teaspoon dried thyme

salt and freshly ground pepper

½ cup (2 oz/60 g) freshly grated
   Parmesan cheese

This recipe is ideal when you have a variety of vegetables on hand, as many different types can be used. Add yellow squash in place of the zucchini or a red or yellow bell pepper in place of the green one. Serve the gratin with a loaf of crusty bread on the side.

Pick over the chick-peas and discard any misshapen peas or stones. Rinse the chick-peas and drain. Place in a bowl, add plenty of water to cover and let soak for 3 hours.

Drain the chick-peas and place in a saucepan with water to cover by 2 inches (5 cm). Bring to a boil, reduce the heat to low and simmer, uncovered, until tender, 45–60 minutes. Drain and set aside.

In a large frying pan over medium heat, warm the olive oil. Add the onions and bell pepper and cook, stirring occasionally, until soft, about 10 minutes. Add the eggplants and zucchini and continue to cook, stirring occasionally, until just lightly browned, about 10 minutes longer. Add the garlic and cook, stirring, for 1 minute. Increase the heat to high and add the tomatoes, vegetable stock, red pepper flakes, basil, thyme and chick-peas. Bring to a boil over high heat. Reduce the heat to medium-low and simmer, uncovered, for 30 minutes. Season to taste with salt and pepper.

Position a rack in the upper third of an oven and preheat to 375°F (190°C). Oil a shallow 2-qt (2-l) baking dish.

Pour the vegetable mixture into the prepared dish. Sprinkle the Parmesan cheese evenly over the top. Bake until golden and bubbling around the edges, about 20 minutes.

Let cool for 10 minutes. Spoon onto warmed plates and serve.

Serves 6

Spicy Grilled Eggplant

9 slender (Asian) eggplants (aubergines)
  or 2 small globe eggplants, about 2 lb
  (1 kg) total weight
salt
6 tablespoons (3 fl oz/90 ml) olive oil
freshly ground pepper
3 cloves garlic, minced
1 tablespoon red wine vinegar
¼ teaspoon red pepper flakes
2 tablespoons chopped fresh parsley

Serve this dish as a first course with wedges of feta cheese and Kalamata olives or as a tasty side dish. If a charcoal grill is unavailable, bake the eggplants in the oven: Oil a baking sheet and arrange the eggplant slices on it in a single layer. Bake on the top rack of a 400°F (200°C) oven, turning occasionally, until golden on both sides, about 15 minutes.

Prepare a fire in a charcoal grill.

Cut the eggplants crosswise into slices ¼ inch (6 mm) thick. If you are using globe eggplants, place the slices in a colander and salt them liberally to draw out the moisture. Let stand for 30 minutes. Rinse with water and pat dry with paper towels. If you are using slender eggplants, there is no need to salt them.

Brush the eggplant slices with 4 tablespoons (2 fl oz/60 ml) of the olive oil. Season to taste with salt and pepper.

When the fire is ready, place the eggplant slices on the grill rack and grill, turning occasionally, until they are tender and golden, 10–12 minutes.

Meanwhile, in a small bowl, stir together the garlic, the remaining 2 tablespoons olive oil and the vinegar.

Place the eggplant on a serving platter and drizzle the garlic-oil mixture over the top. Sprinkle with the red pepper flakes and parsley and serve.

Serves 6

MUSHROOMS

With their meaty textures and rich, earthy flavors, mushrooms are used in many vegetarian dishes. Cultivated white and brown mushrooms are among the most common. In their smallest form, with their caps still closed, they are often called button mushrooms. Chanterelles are subtly flavored wild mushrooms, usually pale yellow, trumpet-shaped and about 2–3 inches (5–7.5 cm) in length. Shiitakes are meaty-flavored Asian mushrooms about 2–3 inches (5–7.5 cm) in diameter that have flat, dark brown caps. Porcini, the widely used Italian name for *Boletus edulis* (also known by the French term *cèpes*), are popular wild mushrooms with a rich, meaty flavor. Rare, honeycomb-textured morels are highly prized for their flavor and aroma, with the dark brown or black variety considered finer in taste and scent than paler ones. Many wild mushroom varieties are available both fresh or dried.

NUTMEG

Sweet spice that is the hard pit of the fruit of the nutmeg tree. May be bought already ground or, for fresher flavor, whole. Whole nutmegs may be kept inside special nutmeg graters (below), which include hinged flaps that conceal a storage compartment, to grate fresh as needed.

OIL

Oils not only provide a medium in which foods may be browned without sticking, but can also subtly enhance the flavor of many dishes. Extra-virgin olive oil, extracted from olives on the first pressing without use of heat or chemicals, is prized for its pure, fruity taste and golden to pale green hue. Products labeled "pure olive oil," less aromatic and flavorful, may be used for all-purpose cooking. Pale gold peanut oil has a subtle hint of the peanut's richness. Asian sesame oil is made with toasted sesame seeds, resulting in a dark, strong oil used primarily as a flavoring ingredient. Sesame oil is also sometimes the basis for Asian hot chili oil, flavored with the spicy essential oil of hot red chili peppers. Nut oils are reminiscent of the flavor of the nuts from which they were pressed. Vegetable and seed oils, such as safflower, canola and corn oil, are employed for their high cooking temperatures and bland flavor.

OLIVES

Throughout the Mediterranean, ripe black olives are commonly cured in combinations of salt, seasonings, brines, vinegars and oils to produce pungently flavored results. Good-quality cured olives, such as French Niçoise (at left) and Greek Kalamata (below), can be found in most well-stocked food stores. To pit an olive, use a special olive pitter, which grips the olive and pushes out the pit in one squeeze. Or use a small, sharp knife to slit the olive lengthwise down to the pit, then pry away the flesh.

ONIONS

All manner of onions are used in vegetarian cooking as featured ingredients or to enhance the flavor of other vegetables. Green onions (below), also called spring onions or scallions, are harvested immature, leaves and all, before their bulbs have formed. The green and white parts may both be enjoyed, raw or cooked, for their mild but still pronounced onion flavor.

Red (Spanish) onions are a mild, sweet variety of onion with purplish red skin and red-tinged white flesh. White-skinned, white-fleshed onions tend to be sweet and mild. Yellow onions are a common, white-fleshed, strong-flavored variety distinguished by their dry, yellowish brown skins. Small but pungent pearl onions about ¾ inch (2 cm) in diameter, also known as pickling onions, are sometimes added whole as an ingredient in vegetable stews and braises.

OREGANO

Aromatic, pungent and spicy Mediterranean herb—also known as wild marjoram—used fresh or dried to season savory dishes.

PAPRIKA

Powdered spice derived from the dried paprika pepper and available in sweet, mild and hot forms.

PITA BREAD

Flat, oval, yeast-leavened bread of Mediterranean origin, noteworthy for the pocket that it forms during baking, making pita ideal for filling as a sandwich. Often served with dips or other appetizers.

PASTAS, DRIED

All pasta should be cooked in ample quantities of boiling water until *al dente*—tender but still chewy—following manufacturer's suggested cooking time. More than 400 distinct commercial pasta shapes exist. Some of the more common ones, used in this book, include:

Farfalle "Butterflies." Also called bow ties.

Fusilli Short, twisted strands, also known as *eliche* or *spirali,* as well as long, twisted strands.

Lasagne Broad, flat ribbons, most often layered with cheese, sauce and other fillings in baked pasta.

Orzo Small, rice-shaped pasta.

Penne "Quills." Tubes of regular or spinach pasta with angled ends resembling pen nibs. Available smooth and ridged (*rigate*).

Macaroni Small to medium short, curved tubes.

POLENTA
Italian term for a cooked cornmeal mush, as well as the coarsely ground cornmeal from which it is made.

RED PEPPER FLAKES
Coarsely ground flakes of dried red chilies, including seeds, that add moderately hot flavor to the foods they season.

RICE
The most popular variety is long-grain white rice, whose slender kernels steam to a light, fluffy consistency. Basmati rice is prized for its slender form, aromatic scent and flavor. Brown rice is rice from which only the outer husk has been removed during milling, leaving a nutritious, fiber-rich coating of bran that gives the grain its distinctive color, chewy texture and nutlike flavor. Wild rice is actually a wild grain. Its unpolished dark brown kernels have a rich flavor and texture that are often compared to that of nuts.

ROMAINE LETTUCE
Popular variety of lettuce with elongated, pale green leaves characterized by their crisp texture and slightly pungent flavor. Also called cos lettuce.

SAFFRON
Intensely aromatic, golden orange spice made from the dried stigmas of a species of crocus; used to perfume and color many classic Mediterranean and East Indian dishes. Sold either as threads—the dried stigmas—or in powdered form. Look for products labeled "pure" saffron.

SHERRY
Fortified, cask-aged wine, ranging from dry to sweet, enjoyed as an aperitif and used as a flavoring in both savory dishes and desserts.

SOY SAUCE
Asian seasoning and condiment made from soybeans, wheat, salt and water.

SUGAR SNAP PEAS
Distinctive pea notable for its sweet flavor, crisp texture, and the fact that it is eaten whole—pod, peas and all—at its peak during spring and autumn. Some types of sugar snap peas are stringless. Others, however, require stringing, simply accomplished by snapping each pod at its leafy end and pulling downward to strip away the string along its edges.

SWISS CHARD
A leafy, dark green vegetable with thick, crisp white or red stems and ribs. The green part, often trimmed from the stems and ribs, may be cooked like spinach, and has a somewhat milder flavor. Also known as silverbeet.

TAHINI
Smooth, rich paste ground from sesame seeds and used in Middle Eastern cooking to enrich the flavor and texture of both savory and sweet dishes. Sold in jars or cans in ethnic markets and well-stocked food stores.

THYME
Fragrant, clean-tasting, small-leaved herb popular fresh or dried as a seasoning.

TOMATILLOS
The green tomatillo resembles, but is not related to, the tomato. Fresh tomatillos usually come encased in brown papery husks, which are easily peeled off before the tomatillos are used. Canned tomatillos can be found in specialty-food sections of most markets.

TOMATOES
During summer, when tomatoes are in season, use the best sun-ripened tomatoes you can find. At other times of the year, plum tomatoes, sometimes called Roma or egg tomatoes, are likely to have the best flavor and texture; canned whole or crushed plum tomatoes are also good. Small red or yellow cherry tomatoes, barely bigger than the fruit for which they are descriptively named, also have a fresh pronounced flavor.

TURMERIC
Pungent, earthy-flavored ground spice that, like **saffron**, adds a vibrant yellow color to any dish.

VINEGARS
Literally "sour wine," vinegar results when certain strains of yeast cause wine—or some other alcoholic liquid such as apple cider or Japanese rice wine—to ferment for a second time, turning it acidic. The best-quality wine vinegars begin with good-quality wine. Red wine vinegar, like the wine from which it is made, has a more robust flavor than vinegar produced from white wine. Balsamic vinegar, a specialty of Modena, Italy, is a vinegar made from reduced grape juice and aged for many years.

ZUCCHINI
Slender, tube-shaped relative of the squash, with edible green, yellow or green-and-cream-striped skin and pale, tender flesh. Also referred to as summer squash or courgette. Look for smaller-sized squashes, which have a finer texture and flavor and less pronounced seeds than many of the larger ones.

ZEST
Thin, brightly colored, outermost layer of a citrus fruit's peel, containing most of its aromatic essential oils—a lively source of flavor. Zest may be removed using one of two easy methods:

1. Use a simple tool known as a zester, drawing its sharp-edged holes across the fruit's skin to remove the zest in thin strips. Alternatively, use the fine holes on a hand-held grater.

2. Holding the edge of a paring knife or vegetable peeler almost parallel to the fruit's skin, carefully cut off the zest in thin strips, taking care not to remove any white pith with it. Then thinly slice or chop on a cutting board.

Index

ACKNOWLEDGMENTS

The publishers would like to thank the following people and organizations
for their generous assistance and support in producing this book:
Jean Tenanes, Alexandra Regos, Paul Weir, Sharon C. Lott, Stephen W. Griswold, Ken DellaPenta,
Stephani Grant, Tina Schmitz, the buyers and store managers for Pottery Barn and Williams-Sonoma stores.

The following kindly lent props for the photography: Biordi Art Imports, Candelier, Fredericksen Hardware,
Fillamento, Forrest Jones, Mariner & Myers Flowers, Sue Fisher King, RH Shop and Chuck Williams.